AQA GCSE Exam Guide

Carole Shepherd   Derek Aust

OXFORD
UNIVERSITY PRESS

The Publisher would like to thank the following for permission to reproduce photographs: Authors: pp.11, 12, 23, 31, 45.

The authors would like to thank their families for their helpful support, suggestions and encouragement, in particular Vasilija Aust and Caterina McKillop.

The Publisher would like to thank Luisa Carrer (language consultant).

OXFORD
UNIVERSITY PRESS

Great Clarendon Street, Oxford OX2 6DP

Oxford University Press is a department of the University of Oxford.
It furthers the University's objective of excellence in research, scholarship, and education by publishing worldwide in

Oxford New York
Auckland Cape Town Dar es Salaam Hong Kong Karachi
Kuala Lumpur Madrid Melbourne Mexico City Nairobi
New Delhi Shanghai Taipei Toronto

With offices in

Argentina Austria Brazil Chile Czech Republic France Greece
Guatemala Hungary Italy Japan South Korea Poland Portugal
Singapore Switzerland Thailand Turkey Ukraine Vietnam

Oxford is a registered trade mark of Oxford University Press
in the UK and in certain other countries

British Library Cataloguing in Publication Data

Data available

ISBN 978 019 913514 1

3 5 7 9 10 8 6 4

Designed and typeset by John Dickinson – Design for Print

Printed and bound by Martins the Printers, Berwick upon Tweed, UK.

Contents ■■■■■

How to use this booklet

The *Amici* coursebook and workbook really provide all that you need to get a good grade in Italian GCSE, provided you use them wisely! This *Amici* Exam Guide gives you extra practice in Listening and Reading, and useful expressions for you to use in Speaking and Writing tasks for AQA examinations It also reminds you of useful pages in the *Amici* coursebook. The *AQA Contexts and Purposes* (topics) listed in this booklet apply to all four skills, although for Speaking and Writing you may choose a context/purpose of your own.

Speaking and Writing

As Speaking and Writing tasks will be set by your teachers, we thought you would find it useful to have a list of some important words/ expressions from *Amici* listed under the *AQA Contexts and Purposes* headings. Remember: once you start preparing your tasks, your teacher cannot give you any help, so it is important you know where to find help in *Amici*. AQA states that *"differentiation is by outcome, not by task"*. This means that you need to show you know appropriate task-related grammar, vocabulary and expressions. A full list of the vocabulary and expressions used in *Amici* (in Italian and English) can also be found at the following website: www.oup.com/oxed/secondary/mfl/amici/

Listening and Reading

You will be entered for either Foundation or Higher examinations. In this booklet, tasks are identified as **F** (Foundation), **H** (Higher) or **F/H** (Foundation/Higher), but we recommend you try all of the activities so that you get lots of practice with different vocabulary and tasks.

To help with your revision for the Listening examinations we have chosen a selection of recordings from *Amici* which relate to the AQA contexts and created different exercises to go with them. For revision purposes you have personal control of the CD included with this exam guide, so will be able to listen as many times as you like. You will be able to check your answers in the back of this booklet, but please make sure you do this AFTER you have done the exercise! All the transcripts are included on the CD ROM.

The Reading comprehension texts and exercises are all new but you should recognise some of the vocabulary. These texts have also been selected to give you some additional useful expressions to help you with your Speaking and Writing tasks. For advice on how to adapt a text refer to *Amici* (page 138).

Icons

AQA uses lots of visual icons in Listening and Reading examination papers, but we do not have enough space to include these here. Instead, you have a good range of exercise types to practise. Ask your teacher to give you some AQA past papers so that you can get used to the icons they use at AQA!

AQA Requirements

Unit 1: Listening

Foundation Tier: 30 minutes (+ 5 minutes reading time) / Higher Tier: 40 minutes (+ 5 minutes reading time)

You are given 5 minutes reading time at the beginning of the test to read the questions. Then you will hear each item twice and there will be a range of question types, including non-verbal responses or responses in English. You will be allowed to make notes during the test. Some items may include reference to past, present and future events and some unfamiliar language. You will be expected to identify main points and extract details and points of view.

Unit 2: Reading

Foundation Tier: 30 minutes / Higher Tier: 50 minutes

There will be a range of question types, including non-verbal responses or responses in English. The tests will include short items e.g. instructions, advertisements, and some longer extracts from brochures, guides, letters, newspapers, magazines, books, faxes, email and websites. The texts may include reference to past, present and future events and some unfamiliar language. You will be expected to use your knowledge of grammar to show you have understood the main message and some details, including points of view, attitudes and emotions.

Unit 3: Speaking

Controlled Assessment – 30% (internally assessed)

Two tasks will be set and marked by your teacher and submitted to AQA for moderation. Both tasks will be in the form of a dialogue. Once you have been given the task your teacher cannot give you any further support, but you will have access to reference materials, including dictionaries, coursebooks and internet resources. You cannot submit the same task for both Speaking and Writing.

Unit 4: Writing

Controlled Assessment – 30% (externally assessed)

You have to complete two controlled assessment tasks which will be set by your teachers but marked by AQA examiners. You must complete all work independently. Once you have been given the task, your teacher cannot give you any further help, but you can refer to reference materials (dictionaries, coursebooks and internet resources). Finally, you will have a maximum of 60 minutes to write up the final version of each task under supervision and you will have access to a dictionary.

If you are aiming at grades G–D you should write approximately 200–350 words across the two tasks; for grades C–A* you should write approximately 400–600 words across the two tasks.

Health

1.1 Healthy and unhealthy lifestyles and their consequences

Quando ero più giovane
Volevo mantenermi in forma
Camminavo ogni giorno
Mi piaceva fare footing
Andavo in palestra
Giocavo a calcio
Andavo in piscina

When I was younger
I wanted to keep fit
I used to walk every day
I used to like jogging
I used to go to the gym
I used to play football
I used to go to the pool

Adesso
Ho cominciato a giocare a …
Ho smesso di giocare a …
Ho smesso di fumare
Non gioco più a calcio
Non vado più in palestra
A colazione mangio poco

Now
I started playing …
I stopped playing …
I have stopped smoking
I no longer play football
I no longer go to the gym
I don't eat much breakfast

Per tenermi in forma …
Sto attento alla dieta
Bevo molta acqua
Cerco di evitare i cibi grassi
Mangio frutta e verdura
Vado in bicicletta
Faccio molto sport
Non vado a letto tardi
Non bevo alcolici
Non fumo (più)

To keep myself fit …
I look after my diet
I drink a lot of water
I try to avoid fatty foods
I eat fruit and vegetables
I go by bicycle
I do a lot of sport
I don't go to bed late
I don't drink alcohol
I don't smoke (any more)

In futuro
Andrò in palestra
Farò aerobica
Mangerò più frutta

In the future
I'll go to the gym
I'll do aerobics
I'll eat more fruit

Try adding one of these expressions of time:

una volta alla settimana	*once a week*
due volte al mese	*twice a month*
due ore al giorno	*two hours a day*
durante la settimana	*during the week*
ogni giorno/sera	*every day/evening*
ogni venerdì	*every Friday*
ogni tanto	*every now and then*
ogni due o tre giorni	*every two or three days*
qualche volta	*sometimes*
spesso	*often*

e.g. Mi mantengo **spesso** in forma. Andavo in palestra **una volta alla settimana**.

➔ Useful pages in *Amici*: 20–25, 41, 106–109

1. ☐ Read the comments about people's lifestyles. **(F)**

Mangiare sano, vivere meglio!

Antonio: mangio sempre prodotti biologici, frutta e verdura a volontà, pasta, riso, insalata e poca carne.

Elena: cerco di mangiare un po' di frutta e verdura ogni giorno perché so che mi fa bene ma poi mi piacciono tanto le patatine, il cioccolato, gli hamburger ...

Giorgio: non seguo una dieta sana e non pratico nessuno sport ma sono contento lo stesso.

Clara: vado sempre a scuola a piedi perché mi piace tanto camminare. Durante l'intervallo mangio una mela o una banana, mai le caramelle o le patatine.

Enrico: non pratico nessuno sport da tanti anni e sono diventato veramente pigro perché vado dappertutto in macchina. Quanto alla dieta, mangio tutte le cose che per la salute non dovrei mangiare.

What is the attitude of these people to a healthy lifestyle? Write **P** (positive), **N** (negative) or **P+N** (positive and negative).

	Person	Letter
Example:	Antonio	*P*
(a)	Elena	
(b)	Giorgio	
(c)	Clara	
(d)	Enrico	

2. Listen to this information about Cristina (CD track 2). Complete the table. **(H)**

Example:	Place of work	*Office*
(a)	**Two** after-work activities	
(b)	How she learned about diet	
(c)	Her everyday diet	
(d)	Main meal preference	

3. Listen to Luisa's conversation with her friend (CD track 3) and answer the following questions. **(H)**

(a) What was Luisa's attitude to sport at school?
(b) Who does she thank for her recent interest in sport and why?
(c) What **two** activities does she now do and how often?
(d) What **two** things did she use to eat for breakfast?
(e) What does she regularly drink for breakfast?
(f) How has her attitude to food and drink changed?

Relationships and Choices

1.2 Relationships with family and friends

Come ti chiami?	Mi chiamo …
Qual è il tuo cognome?	Il mio cognome è …
Di che nazionalità sei?	Sono *italiano*
Quando è il tuo compleanno?	Il mio compleanno è …
Quanti anni hai?	Ho … anni
Quando sei nato/a?	Sono nato/a nel …
Dove sei nato/a?	Sono nato/a a …
Dove abiti?	Abito a …
Qual è il tuo numero di cellulare?	Il mio numero è …
Qual è il tuo indirizzo (e-mail)?	Il mio indirizzo è …

Family members

la famiglia	*family*
il bambino	*baby, child*
la bambina	*baby, child*
il/la cugino/a	*cousin*
il/la figlio/a	*son/daughter*
il fratellastro	*half-brother*
il fratello	*brother*
il/la gemello/a	*twin (m/f)*
i genitori	*parents*
la madre	*mother*
il marito	*husband*
la moglie	*wife*
la nonna	*grandmother*
il nonno	*grandfather*
il nipote	*nephew*
la nipote	*niece*
i nonni	*grandparents*
il padre	*father*
i parenti	*relations*
il ragazzo	*boy*
la ragazza	*girl*
la sorella	*sister*
la sorellastra	*half-sister*
la zia	*aunt*
lo zio	*uncle*

Colours

azzurro	*blue*
bianco	*white*
biondo	*blonde*
castano	*brown*
celeste	*blue*
blu (inv)	*blue*
grigio	*grey*
nero	*black*
rosso	*red*
verde	*green*

Descriptions

alto	*tall*
i baffi	*moustache*
la barba	*beard*
basso	*small (height)*
bello	*beautiful*
brutto	*ugly*
calvo	*bald*
i capelli	*hair*
corto	*short*
grasso	*fat*
grosso	*big*
le lenti a contatto	*contact lenses*
liscio	*straight (hair)*
lungo (lunghi)	*long*
magro/snello	*thin/slim*
gli occhi	*eyes*
gli occhiali	*glasses*
ondulato	*wavy*
gli orecchini	*earrings*
i ricci	*curls*

Character

allegro / felice	*happy*
amichevole	*friendly*
antipatico	*not nice*
chiacchierone/a	*chatterbox*
contento	*happy*
divertente	*amusing*
gentile	*kind*
intelligente	*intelligent*
interessante	*interesting*
noioso	*boring*
pigro	*lazy*
simpatico	*nice*
stupido	*stupid*
timido	*shy, timid*
vivace	*lively*

➔ Useful pages in *Amici*: 14–19, 140–141

1. ⬚⬚ Read about Matteo's and Francesca's families. **(F/H)**

> Fratelli! Che sarebbe la mia famiglia senza di loro? Io sono il mezzano, nel senso che ho un fratello più grande e una sorella più piccola e anche se qualche volta litighiamo, io li amo da morire! **Matteo**
>
> Sì sono d'accordo ... è stupendo avere un fratello o una sorella anche perché per tutta la vita avremo una persona su cui poter contare ... sì, sono davvero contenta di non essere figlia unica, anche perché con un fratello e una sorella impari moltissimo, impari a non essere egoista, ma a condividere, impari ad essere una persona migliore ... **Francesca**

Answer the following questions. Write **M** (Matteo), **F** (Francesca), **M+F** (Matteo and Francesca) or **N** (Neither).

(a) Who is happy not to be an only child? ⬚

(b) Who has a brother and a sister? ⬚

(c) Who quarrels all the time? ⬚

(d) Who has a younger sister? ⬚

(e) Who adopts a negative attitude to their brother or sister? ⬚

(f) Who will learn not to be selfish? ⬚

2. 🎧 Listen to Lorenzo (CD track 4) and complete the table. **(F)**

(a)	Girlfriend's name	
(b)	Age	
(c)	Number of brothers and sisters	
(d)	Place of birth	
(e)	Character	

3. 🎧 Listen to the dialogues (CD track 5) and choose a word from the list that best describes each person. Write the correct letter in the table. **(H)**

	Person	Letter
(a)	Stefano	
(b)	Germana	
(c)	Sonia	
(d)	Marinella	
(e)	Roberto	
(f)	Filippo	

A pessimist
B egoist
C honest
D spoilt
E inquisitive
F optimist
G ambitious
H lazy
I perfectionist

1.3 Future plans regarding marriage/partnership

In passato le ragazze si sposavano molto giovani	*In the past girls married very young*
Era il ruolo del marito mantenere la famiglia	*It was the husband's role to maintain the family*
La moglie stava a casa, faceva le faccende domestiche e si occupava dei figli	*The wife stayed at home, did the household chores and looked after the children*
Adesso le ragazze desiderano farsi una carriera	*Now girls want to have a career*
Molte ragazze di 30 anni non hanno figli	*Many girls of 30 have no children*
Ci sono molte coppie sposate senza figli	*There are many married couples without children*
Ci sono più famiglie monogenitoriali	*There are more one-parent families*
È aumentato anche il numero dei divorzi	*The number of divorces has also increased*
Molti giovani preferiscono convivere	*Many young people prefer to live together*
Hai intenzione di sposarti?	*Do you intend to get married?*
Vuoi avere bambini?	*Do you want to have children?*
Secondo te, qual è l'età ideale per sposarsi?	*In your opinion, what's the ideal age to get married?*
Come sarà il futuro sposo/la futura sposa?	*What will your future bridegroom/ bride be like?*
Ho intenzione di sposarmi all'età di ...	*I intend to get married at the age of ...*
Non ho nessuna intenzione di sposarmi	*I have no intention of getting married*
Vorrei avere ... bambini	*I'd like to have ... children*
(Non) mi piacerebbe avere più di due figli	*I'd (not) like to have more than two children*
Secondo me, l'età ideale per sposarsi è ... anni	*In my opinion the ideal age to get married is ...*
Non penso che ci sia un'età giusta o sbagliata	*I don't think that there is a right or a wrong age*
Il mio futuro sposo/la mia futura sposa sarà ...	*My future bridegroom/bride will be ...*

➜ Useful pages in *Amici*: 144, 198

1. ⬚⬚ Read Susanna's and Luisa's e-mails about marriage. (H)

Per sposarsi non penso che ci sia un'età giusta o sbagliata, penso sia più una questione di persona giusta o sbagliata! Però diciamo che io sinceramente anche se incontrassi l'uomo della mia vita non mi sposerei prima dei trent'anni! Al momento la mia carriera è più importante.
Susanna

Pensavo di sposarmi a un'età giovane, ma adesso ho cambiato idea perché voglio andare all'università. Un giorno vorrei anche avere figli e mi rendo conto che più una donna è avanti con l'età più sorgono complicazioni ...! Comunque, penso che, potendo scegliere, aspetterei fino a dopo il matrimonio per avere dei figli!
Luisa

According to the e-mails which of the following statements are: **T** (true), **F** (false), **?** (not in the text)?

(a) The age you get married doesn't matter. ☐

(b) I would get married in my 20s if I met the right man. ☐

(c) My current job pays well. ☐

(d) I have decided to continue studying rather than to marry young. ☐

(e) I would like to have two or three children. ☐

(f) Having children when you are older is not a problem. ☐

(g) Given the choice I would have children before getting married. ☐

2. 🎧 Listen to the conversation between Daniela and Elena (CD track 6) and answer the following questions in English. (H)

(a) When does Daniela want to get married?

(b) What does she want to do before getting married?

(c) How is Marco described?

(d) What exactly does Daniela say about children?

1.4 Social Issues and equality

l'AIDS	*AIDS*
l'atto di violenza	*act of violence*
la beneficenza	*charity*
la discriminazione etnica	*ethnic discrimination*
la discriminazione razziale	*racial discrimination*
gli extracomunitari	*people from outside the EU*
l'immigrato	*immigrant*
minacciare	*to threaten*
onesto	*honest*
povero	*poor*
la povertà	*poverty*
il pregiudizio	*prejudice*
la prostituzione	*prostitution*
il razzismo	*racism*
il teppismo	*hooliganism*
il teppista	*hooligan*
il sieropositivo	*HIV positive*
l'uguaglianza	*equality*
umiliato	*humiliated*
il vandalismo	*vandalism*
la xenofobia	*xenophobia*

i graffiti

Ai giovani il fumo fa malissimo	*Smoking is very bad for youngsters*
Danneggia i polmoni	*It damages the lungs*
È molto difficile smettere	*It's very difficult to stop*
La droga causa problemi	*Drugs cause problems*
L'alcol può provocare gravi danni al fegato	*Alcohol can cause serious liver damage*
Molti immigrati si sentono umiliati e minacciati	*Many immigrants feel humiliated and threatened*
C'è il problema dell'inserimento sociale	*There is the problem of integration into society*
Bisogna rispettare se stessi	*You must respect yourself*
Essere volontari è un lavoro molto impegnativo	*It's a time-consuming job being a volunteer*
Bisogna ascoltare i bisogni dell'altro	*You need to listen to the needs of others*
Hai mai fatto un lavoro di volontariato?	*Have you ever worked as a volunteer?*
Che cosa si fa nella tua città per aiutare i senzatetto?	*What does your town do to help the homeless?*
Porti cose ad un negozio di beneficenza?	*Do you take things to a charity shop?*

→ Useful pages in *Amici*: 162–167, 201

1. ⬛ Read the passage about the living conditions of immigrants and complete the table. (**H**)

> C'è chi dorme in garage, chi vive in dieci in un locale. Tanti sono gli immigrati che hanno difficoltà a trovare casa o alloggio nel nostro Paese. I dati nazionali parlano chiaro: solo l'11,8% degli immigrati presenti in Italia è proprietario di casa. Oltre il 72% è in affitto, mentre il 16,1% "vive in condizioni abitative precarie". Più precisamente, il 7,5% vive in casa di parenti e amici, il 6,8% accampato sul luogo di lavoro. Non è tutto. Del 72% di immigrati che stanno in affitto, quasi il 20% si trova in condizioni di "grave sovraffollamento". In numeri assoluti significa che, mentre un milione e mezzo di immigrati vanta condizioni abitative stabili, circa 900mila vivono nell'"area del disagio": un esercito di senza tetto e senza diritti.

	Immigrants who ...	%
(a)	sleep at their place of work.	
(b)	live in rented accommodation.	
(c)	own their own home.	
(d)	live with family and friends.	
(e)	live in seriously overcrowded rented accommodation.	

2. 🎧 Listen to Gianpaolo interviewing a young boy about smoking (CD track 7) and complete the sentences. (**F**)

(a) Ezio is _____ years old.

(b) He hasn't smoked for _____.

(c) He smoked for _____.

(d) Giving up was _____.

(e) He used to smoke _____.

3. 🎧 Listen to the rest of the conversation (CD track 8) and answer the following questions in English. (**H**)

(a) What did Ezio do first when he stopped smoking?

(b) What sort of company was he happy with and why?

(c) What did he also find helped him and why?

(d) In what other way did giving up smoking help him?

(e) Why does Ezio mention money?

A quick reminder:

Nouns

Italian nouns end in **-o**, **-a** or **-e**.
In the plural these endings change as follows:

-o	-i
-a	-e
-e	-i

libro ⟶ libri
penna ⟶ penne
cellulare ⟶ cellulari

Adjectives

Italian adjectives ending in **-o** have four forms. Those ending in **-e** have two forms.

-o	-i
-a	-e
-e	-i

italiano ⟶ italiani
italiana ⟶ italiane
inglese ⟶ inglesi

NB: tedesco/a ⟶ tedeschi/e

The present tense

Regular verb infinitives end in **-are**, **-ere** or **-ire**.

-are	-ere	-ire (1)	-ire (2)
-o	-o	-o	-isco
-i	-i	-i	-isci
-a	-e	-e	-isce
-iamo	-iamo	-iamo	-iamo
-ate	-ete	-ite	-ite
-ano	-ono	-ono	-iscono

NB: **-care** and **-gare** verbs add an 'h' before 'e' or 'i':
cercare ⟶ cerco, cerchi etc.;
pagare ⟶ pago, paghi etc.

-iare verbs drop the 'i' in the **tu** form unless it is stressed:
viaggiare ⟶ viaggi;
cominciare ⟶ cominci; but sciare: scii.

The perfect tense

For the perfect tense you need the present tense of **avere (ho, hai, ha, abbiamo, avete, hanno)** or **essere** and the past participle of the verb.
For the past participle of regular verbs, take off the **-are**, **-ere** or **-ire** and add the ending:

-are	-ato	lavorare	⟶	lavorato
-ere	-uto	vendere	⟶	venduto
-ire	-ito	finire	⟶	finito

Most verbs take **avere (ho, hai, ha, abbiamo, avete, hanno)**
e.g. **ho lavorato, ho venduto, ho finito**.

Some verbs take **essere (sono, sei, è, siamo, siete, sono)**
e.g. andare, arrivare, essere (stato), nascere (nato), morire (morto), piacere (piaciuto), rimanere (rimasto), stare, uscire, venire (venuto).

The past participle of verbs taking **essere** agrees with the subject
e.g. Marco: "sono andato", Daniela: "sono andata"; i miei amici sono andati; le mie amiche sono andate.

The imperfect tense

To form the imperfect, remove the **-re** of the infinitive and add:
-vo, -vi, -va, -vamo, -vate, -vano e.g. stavo; avevo; finivo.

NB: **fare**: facevo; facevi; faceva; facevamo; facevate; facevano.

essere: ero; eri; era; eravamo; eravate; erano.

➔ Useful pages in *Amici*: 26–27, 68–69, 210–217, 225–227

Expressing the future

As in English, there are many ways of avoiding the future tense in Italian, e.g. use the present tense or an expression such as **Ho intenzione di/ Spero di/Vorrei.**
Ho intenzione di sposarmi all'età di 30 anni.
Spero di avere due bambini. Vorrei vivere in Italia.

The future tense

The future endings are: **-ò, -ai, -à, -emo, -ete, -anno.**

Regular **-ere** and **-ire** verbs form the future tense 'stem' by removing the final 'e' of the infinitive. Regular **-are** verbs change the 'a' of the infinitive to 'e': parlar —→ parler.

parlare	parlerò	parlerai	parlerà	parleremo	parlerete	parleranno
vendere	venderò	venerai	venderà	venderemo	venderete	venderanno
finire	finirò	finirai	finirà	finiremo	finirete	finiranno

NB: **-care** and **-gare** verbs add an 'h' throughout:
cercare —→ cercherò etc.; pagare —→ pagherò etc.

-giare verbs and most **-ciare** verbs drop the 'i':
viaggiare —→ viaggerò; cominciare —→ comincerò

A number of verbs have the same endings but a different "stem":
andare —→ andrò; fare —→ farò; potere —→ potrò.

The only completely irregular verb stem is **essere**:
sarò, sarai, sarà, saremo, sarete, saranno.

The conditional tense

The conditional tense has the same "stem" as the future but these endings: **-ei, -esti, -ebbe, -emmo, -este, -ebbero.**

Any verb which is irregular in the future will also be irregular in the conditional
e.g. **essere: sarei, saresti, sarebbe, saremmo, sareste, sarebbero.**

e.g. Mangio tutto quello che non **dovrei** mangiare.
Vorrei mangiare più frutta.
Mi piacerebbe andare in palestra.

→ Useful pages in *Amici*: 48, 116–117, 217, 225–227

aiuto !

When preparing for your Writing or Speaking tasks, try to use a variety of tenses, time expressions, vocabulary and adjectives. Adapt the sentences in this Chapter, e.g.

Andavo spesso in palestra.	past
Vado in piscina ogni giorno.	present
Andrò allo stadio giovedì prossimo.	future

Free Time and the Media

2.1 Free time activities

Preferisco il calcio	*I prefer football*
Odio giocare a calcio	*I hate playing football*
Mi piace giocare a hockey	*I like to play hockey*
Guardo la partita allo stadio	*I watch the match at the stadium*
Preferisco guardare la partita alla televisione	*I prefer watching the match on television*
Non mi piace andare a cavallo	*I don't like horse riding*
Detesto andare in palestra	*I hate going to the gym*
Odio andare al centro sportivo	*I hate going to the sports centre*
È fantastico	*It's fantastic*
È molto interessante	*It's very interesting*
È abbastanza pericoloso	*It's quite dangerous*
È un po' noioso	*It's a little boring*

Mi piace ... — *I like ...*

giocare nel parco	*playing in the park*
giocare a carte	*playing cards*
suonare la chitarra	*playing the guitar*
ascoltare la musica	*listening to music*
guardare la tv	*watching TV*
leggere i giornali, le riviste	*reading papers, magazines*
passeggiare con il cane	*walking the dog*
andare al cinema, a teatro	*going to the cinema, theatre*
andare ai concerti	*going to concerts*
andare in città/disco(teca)	*going to town/the disco*
andare in campagna	*going to the country(side)*
uscire con amici	*going out with friends*

Mi piacciono ... — *I like ...*

i cartoni animati	*cartoons*
i documentari	*documentaries*
i teleromanzi/le telenovele	*TV soaps*
i programmi sportivi	*sports programmes*
i film comici	*comic films*
i film polizieschi	*detective films*
i film romantici	*romantic films*
i film dell'orrore	*horror films*
i film d'avventura	*adventure films*
i film di fantascienza	*science fiction films*

→ Useful pages in *Amici*: 20–25, 120–125, 184

1. 📖 Read what Stefania, Flavio and Marco have to say about their free time. (**F**)

Nel mio tempo libero faccio un po' di tutto: pratico diversi sport, guardo la tv, vado in giro con i miei amici, ascolto musica e suono la chitarra o il pianoforte. A tutti questi hobby dedico molto tempo. **Stefania**

Come passatempi vado su internet per chattare e a volte leggo ma non sono per niente sportivo. A me piace uscire con gli amici per non stare con i miei genitori perché stare con loro è noioso! Andiamo spesso al cinema, non importa quale film danno. **Flavio**

Io dedico poco tempo libero allo sport perché di solito ho troppi compiti. L'unico sport che mi piace è il calcio ma gioco raramente. La mia passione è il cinema ma vado a vedere solo i film di avventura, dell'orrore o di fantascienza. **Marco**

Which of the following people might get on well with Stefania (**S**), Flavio (**F**) or Marco (**M**)?

(a) Ed does not like sports much, but loves watching all sorts of films. ☐

(b) Sarah likes reading and chatting on the Internet. ☐

(c) Antony loves football and science fiction films. ☐

(d) Lyndsey loves playing lots of different sports. ☐

(e) David prefers going out with his friends to spending time with his parents. ☐

2. 🎧 Listen to what Daniela's mother does during the week (CD track 9) and complete the missing information in the grid. (**F/H**)

	When?	Activity?	Where?	With?
(a)	Tuesday evening			
(b)	Wednesday evening			
(c)	Thursday evening			
(d)	Friday morning			
(e)	Friday evening			
(f)	Saturday evening			

3. 🎧 Listen to these dialogues about films (CD track 10) and answer the questions in English. (**H**)

Dialogue 1

(a) What was the film that Ernestina saw about?

(b) What effect did the film have on her and why was this a good thing?

Dialogue 2

(a) What did Alberto like about the film?

(b) Give two negative comments he makes.

2.2 Shopping, money, fashion and trends

i negozi del quartiere	*local shops*
l'edicola	*newsagent's kiosk*
il fruttivendolo	*greengrocer's*
la gelateria	*ice cream shop*
il grande magazzino	*department store*
l'ipermercato (m)	*hypermarket*
la libreria	*bookshop*
la macelleria	*butcher's*
il mercato	*market*
il negozio di abbigliamento	*clothes shop*
il negozio di elettrodomestici	*electrical goods shop*
il negozio di generi alimentari	*food shop, grocer's*
il negozio di mobili	*furniture shop*
il negozio	*shop*
la panetteria	*baker's*
la pasticceria	*cake shop*
la profumeria	*perfumery*
la salumeria	*delicatessen*
il supermercato	*supermarket*
la tabaccheria	*tobacconist's shop*
l'ufficio postale	*post office*
la moda	*fashion*
l'abbigliamento (m)	*clothing*
l'abito	*suit, dress*
andare di moda	*to be in fashion*
la borsa	*bag, handbag*
la calza	*sock, stocking*
i calzini	*socks*
la camicia/camicetta	*shirt/blouse*
il costume da bagno	*bathing costume*
la cravatta	*tie*
la felpa	*sweatshirt*
la giacca	*jacket*
la gonna	*skirt*
i jeans (inv)	*jeans*
la maglia	*jumper*
la maglietta	*t-shirt*
gli orecchini	*earrings*
i pantaloni	*trousers*
il portafoglio	*wallet*
il portamonete (inv)	*purse*
il piercing	*piercing*
il profumo	*perfume*
il pullover (inv)	*pullover*
il sandalo	*sandal*
la scarpa	*shoe*
la sciarpa	*scarf*
lo stivale	*boot*
il tatuaggio	*tattoo*
il vestito	*dress, suit*

→ Useful pages in *Amici*: 126–131, 197

1. ☐☐ Read these opinions about fashion. **(F/H)**

Non mi piace la moda, cerco di andarle contro, ma se un capo mi piace lo compro anche se è alla moda. **Franco**

Dipende da come mi sento ... in genere mi vesto glam, ma sempre con qualche tocco di stravaganza. **Silvana**

Ti dico che il mio concetto di moda è ... se c'è qualcosa che mi piace lo guardo e lo prendo ... non vado certo a spendere però dei milioni per delle cose che non mi piacciono o che non mi stanno per niente bene!! **Barbara**

Conosco le ultime tendenze e so cosa propone la moda ... ma non mi faccio influenzare molto! **Leonardo**

Mi piace fare shopping, magari con qualche amica. Mi piace girare per negozi, provarmi quello che mi piace e comprare tutto ciò che soddisfi il mio ego. L'importante è che sia sempre qualcosa di elegante. **Elvina**

Match the statements to the people. Write **F** (Franco), **S** (Silvana), **B** (Barbara), **L** (Leonardo) or **E** (Elvina).

(a) I buy what I like. ☐

(b) How I dress depends on how I feel. ☐

(c) I enjoy going around the shops. ☐

(d) I am not easily influenced by fashion. ☐

(e) Generally, I don't like fashion. I only buy something fashionable if I like it. ☐

(f) I love really elegant clothes. ☐

(g) I certainly don't spend lots of money buying clothes I don't like. ☐

2. ◯ Listen to the dialogue about Marco in a shop (CD track 11). Complete the table. **(F)**

(a)	Marco wants to buy	
(b)	His size	
(c)	His preferred colour	
(d)	Colour he finally chooses	
(e)	Cost	

3. ☐☐ Listen to the interview with Angela (CD track 12) and answer the questions in English. **(H)**

(a) How long has Angela worked in the shop and who does she work with?

(b) Explain whether the arrival of the shopping centres affected the shop.

(c) What **three** factors have contributed to the success of the supermarkets?

(d) Give **two** disadvantages and **one** advantage of the supermarkets' success.

2.3 Advantages and disadvantages of new technology

anonimo	*anonymous*	il mouse	*mouse*
il beneficio	*benefit*	onesto	*honest*
caricare	*to upload*	il programmatore	*programmer*
la chat	*chatroom*	il rischio	*risk*
il chat server	*chat server*	scaricare	*to download*
chattare	*to chat*	il sito internet	*Internet site*
il destinatario	*recipient*	il sito web	*website*
didattico	*educational*	il soprannome	*nickname*
Grande fratello	*Big Brother*	la tastiera	*keyboard*
meraviglioso	*marvellous*	il tecnico	*technician*
monitorare	*to monitor*	l'utente	*user*

Ho un cellulare da ... Lo uso molto	*I have had a mobile phone since ... I use it a lot*
Preferisco mandare un messaggio che telefonare	*I prefer to send a message than to phone*
Mi piacciono le chatroom	*I like chatrooms*
Passo molto tempo in rete	*I spend a lot of time online*
Il maggiore svantaggio di Internet è ...	*The greatest disadvantage of the Internet is ...*
Il maggiore vantaggio di Internet è ...	*The greatest advantage of the Internet is ...*
Mi piace usare l'Internet	*I like using the Internet*
Uso Internet per ...	*I use the Internet to ...*
Consente di comunicare con persone in luoghi distanti	*It allows you to talk to people in far-off places*
I controlli sono possibili	*Controls are possible*
L'uso della chat ha più rischi che benefici	*Using chatrooms has more risks than benefits*

➔ Useful pages in *Amici*: 86, 169, 192, 202

1. ☐☐ Read about the advantages and disadvantages of the computer and answer the questions in English. (**H**)

Vantaggi:
- ti permette di fare diversi tipi di operazioni che ti fanno risparmiare moltissimo tempo - invio di messaggi di testo in tempo reale, prenotazione di biglietti aerei o ferroviari on line, fare acquisti senza muoverti da casa ecc.
- il telelavoro: è meno costoso lavorare da casa.
- la ricerca di qualsiasi tipo di informazione in modo facile e veloce - basta digitare poche parole chiave su google per trovare le previsioni del tempo, la distanza dell'albergo dall'aeroporto ecc.

Svantaggi:
- il costo e la capacità di utilizzarlo che non tutti hanno, in particolare gli anziani.
- i problemi di salute, per esempio alla schiena, agli occhi ecc.

(a) Give **two** things you can do on the computer that save you lots of time.

(b) What advantages does the computer have for the working person?

(c) What sort of useful research can you do online?

(d) Who might find the computer difficult and why?

(e) What health problems can the computer pose?

2. ◗ Listen to the following extract about the Internet (CD track 13) and complete the sentences. (**F**)

(a) Shopping online is very _____ especially in the _____ .

(b) Now there is also an increase of _____ in Europe.

(c) The percentage of people shopping online in Italy is _____ whereas in _____ it is 47%.

(d) In the UK the figure is _____ and in _____ 65%.

(e) The number of Internet users is predicted to go from 150 to _____ million.

3. ◗ Listen to Daniela, Alessandra and Gianpaolo discussing chatrooms (CD track 14) and answer these questions in English. (**H**)

(a) According to Daniela, what are the main advantages of chatrooms?

(b) What does Alessandra say you might find?

(c) What is Gianpaolo's attitude to chatrooms and why?

Holidays

2.4 Plans, preferences, experiences

Di solito passo una settimana al mare	*Usually I spend a week at the seaside*
Mi sembra una vacanza ideale	*It seems an ideal holiday*
Passo una quindicina di giorni in montagna	*I spend a fortnight in the mountains*
Mi piace stare in albergo	*I like staying in a hotel*
Fare campeggio è meno caro che stare in albergo	*Camping is less expensive than staying in a hotel*
Preferisco affittare un appartamento	*I prefer to rent an apartment*
Vado a trovare amici	*I go to see friends*
Posso rilassarmi	*I can relax*
Ho intenzione di partire verso la fine di agosto	*I intend to leave towards the end of August*
Mi piace fare delle belle passeggiate	*I like going for nice walks*
Mi piace prendere il sole	*I like to sunbathe*
Non vedo l'ora di andare in vacanza	*I can't wait to go on holiday*
C'è qualcosa da fare per persone di tutte le età	*There is something to do for people of all ages*
Sono andato in vacanza con amici	*I went on holiday with friends*
L'estate scorsa ho viaggiato in treno	*Last summer I travelled by train*
Ho fatto campeggio	*I went camping*
Ho incontrato giovani di tutte le parti del mondo	*I met young people from all over the world*
Ho passato il tempo a prendere il sole	*I spent time sunbathing*
Ho visitato tanti musei	*I visited lots of museums*
Ho visto tanto	*I saw so much*
Ho fatto lo sci nautico	*I went water skiing*
Sono andato a pescare ogni giorno	*Every day I went fishing*
Mi sono divertito un mondo	*I really enjoyed myself*
Era fantastico	*It was fantastic*
Faceva bello ma non troppo caldo	*It was nice weather but not too hot*
Se avessi la possibilità di viaggiare andrei in Italia	*If I could travel, I'd go to Italy*
Se fossi ricco farei una bella vacanza	*If I was rich I'd have a lovely holiday*
Mi piacerebbe andare in un'isola disabitata	*I'd like to go to a desert island*

→ Useful pages in *Amici*: 60–77, 180–190

1. Read about Luisella's holiday and then choose the correct response. **(F/H)**

> **Qual è la città italiana più bella che abbiate mai visitato?**
> La più bella che ho visitato ... allora sono belle Firenze, Venezia, Siena ma, secondo me, nessuna batte Roma!
>   Quest'estate sono andata con i miei genitori a Roma. Abbiamo dormito nella nostra vecchia casa. I primi giorni abbiamo visitato il centro storico, poi siamo andati a salutare alcuni amici e per tutto il resto del tempo siamo stati al mare ad Ostia e abbiamo fatto compere. Verso la fine di luglio siamo stati una settimana a Tivoli da alcuni parenti. Sono stata davvero felice perché sono anche riuscita a passare qualche giorno con le mie vecchie compagne di scuola che non vedevo da tanto tempo. **Luisella**

Write the correct letter in the boxes.

(a) Luisella's favourite city is ...
   A Venice.   B Florence.   C Rome. ☐

(b) She went to Rome with her ...
   A relatives.   B parents.   C friends. ☐

(c) They visited the old part of the city ...
   A first.   B on the second last day.   C on the last day. ☐

(d) They went to Tivoli in ...   A June.   B January.   C July. ☐

(e) Luisella saw her old school friends for ...
   A a few days.   B one day.   C a month. ☐

(f) She last saw these school friends ...
   A a week ago.   B a few days ago.   C a long time ago. ☐

2. Listen to Luca (CD track 15) and complete the holiday details. **(F)**

(a)	Country visited	
(b)	With whom	
(c)	Departure date	
(d)	Duration of holiday	
(e)	Mode of transport	
(f)	Comment on holiday	

3. Listen to the dialogue about Roberto's parents' holiday (CD track 16) and write the correct letter in the box. **(H)**

(a) Roberto's parents went to Boston ... ☐
   A for family reasons.   B on a business trip.   C to live.

(b) Roberto's brother is ... ☐
   A at university.   B. looking for a job.   C working.

(c) Roberto's parents remained in Boston ... ☐
   A a month.   B two weeks.   C permanently.

(d) The parents' reaction to the States was ... ☐
   A negative.   B positive.   C positive and negative.

2.5 What to see and getting around

Vorrei noleggiare una bicicletta	*I would like to hire a bicycle*
La vorrei noleggiare per un'ora	*I would like to hire it for one hour*
Preferirei andare in macchina	*I would prefer to go by car*
Al mare non mi annoio mai	*I never get bored at the seaside*
Passo ogni giorno in spiaggia	*I spend every day on the beach*
Faccio il bagno, gioco a pallavolo in spiaggia	*I go for a swim, I play volleyball on the beach*
Alla sera mi piace andare a ballare	*In the evening I like going dancing*
Stare in spiaggia tutto il giorno non mi va	*Staying on the beach all day is not for me*
Durante le mie vacanze amo sciare	*During my holidays I love to ski*
Preferisco andarci durante la stagione sciistica	*I prefer going there during the skiing season*
Mi piace essere circondata dalla neve	*I like to be surrounded by snow*
Mi piace anche noleggiare una macchina	*I also like to hire a car*
Noleggio una bicicletta e vado in giro	*I hire a bike and travel around*
Mi interessa la storia	*I'm interested in history*
Voglio vedere il più possibile	*I want to see as much as possible*
Visito chiese, musei, siti archeologici ecc.	*I visit churches, museums, archeological sites etc.*
Ho noleggiato una barca	*I hired a boat*
Tutti si divertivano un mondo	*Everyone was enjoying themselves*
L'atmosfera era magica	*The atmosphere was magic*
C'era gente che ballava e cantava	*There were people dancing and singing*
Lo spettacolo non finiva mai	*The spectacle was never-ending*
Ero molto fortunato con il tempo	*I was very lucky with the weather*
Meno male che avevo la macchina fotografica	*It's a good job I had my camera*
Ero un po' triste il giorno della partenza	*I was a little sad on the day we were leaving*

➜ Useful pages in *Amici*: 78, 84, 87, 89

1. ▢▢ Read Antonella's e-mail about a trip to Florence. **(F/H)**

> Ciao a tutti, bellissimi i miei tre giorni a Firenze. Due notti passate nella pensione di Elisabetta ed Antonio, simpaticissimi e molto disponibili. Sono arrivata da Genova all'una e mezza e, dopo aver posato la valigia in camera, uno dei due gestori, Antonio, mi ha dato una cartina di Firenze e mi ha consigliato autobus e posti da visitare. Quindi già nel pomeriggio ho fatto una bella camminata visitando la chiesa di Santa Maria Novella, Palazzo Strozzi e Piazza Della Signoria. Il giorno dopo, gustata una meravigliosa colazione, ho visitato ancora una volta Piazza della Signoria, gli Uffizi, Ponte Vecchio e Palazzo Pitti.
>
> L'ultimo giorno sono andato al Duomo e ho fatto un'altra visitina a Piazza Della Signoria. Sono rimasta stupefatta dalle meravigliose opere d'arte e dal gran numero di turisti presenti, soprattutto giapponesi. Ho apprezzato molto le vie del centro storico e le piccole botteghe. Non vi dico quante foto ho scattato!
>
> ***Antonella***

According to Antonella's e-mail, which of the following statements are: **T** (true), **F** (false), **?** (not in the text)?

(a) Antonella spent less than a week in Florence. ▢

(b) Elisabetta and Antonio were not very helpful. ▢

(c) Antonella took a taxi to the hotel. ▢

(d) She bought a map of Florence. ▢

(e) The first afternoon she went around on foot. ▢

(f) She visited Piazza della Signoria more than once. ▢

(g) There were lots of American tourists in Florence. ▢

(h) Unfortunately Antonella didn't take many photos. ▢

2. ◯ Listen to Daniela talking about her trip with Elena (CD track 17) and complete the table. **(F)**

Time of arrival	
Season	
Transport from airport by	
Type of accommodation	
Animals living on Phillip Island	
Distance of island from city	

3. ◯ Listen to Gianni and Elena (CD track 18) and answer the following questions in English. **(H)**

(a) Why is Gianni interested in the notice?

(b) What does Gianni suggest?

(c) Is Elena's reaction positive or negative? Why?

(d) How does Gianni try and convince Elena of his idea?

(e) What are Elena's **two** conditions for accepting?

A quick reminder:

Relative pronouns

A **relative pronoun** refers back to someone/something that has just been mentioned.

1. **che** means who, whom, which, that, and is invariable.
   L'unico sport che mi piace è il calcio.
   The only sport that I like is football.
   Se c'è qualcosa che mi piace lo prendo.
   If there is something I like, I'll get it.

2. **cui** is usually used with a preposition (to/in which, to/from whom etc.) and is invariable.
   Questo è l'albergo in cui ho incontrato i miei amici.
   This is the hotel in which I met my friends.
   Ecco la piazza di cui ti ho parlato.
   Here is the square about which I spoke to you.

3. **cui** can also mean "whose".
   Quella amica, il cui nome non ricordo, è italiana.
   The friend, whose name I do not remember, is Italian.

→ Useful pages in *Amici*: 77, 91

Subjunctive expressions

The present subjunctive is sometimes needed after certain expressions e.g. **Penso che/È importante che:**
Penso che sia una buona idea.
I think it is a good idea.
L'importante è che sia sempre qualcosa di elegante.
The important thing is that it is always elegant.

The imperfect subjunctive is frequently used after **se** (if) to express the idea of something you would like to happen.
Se avessi la possibilità di viaggiare, andrei in Italia.
If I could travel, I'd go to Italy.
Se fossi ricco farei una bella vacanza.
If I was rich I'd have a lovely holiday.

→ Useful pages in *Amici*: 174–175, 219–220, 222

aiuto !

When preparing for your Writing or Speaking tasks, try to use a variety of tenses, time expressions, vocabulary and adjectives. Adapt the sentences in this Chapter, e.g.

Quando ero giovane, l'unico sport che mi piaceva era la pallacanestro.

Penso che la moda italiana sia molto bella.

Se fossi ricco/a andrei a vivere in America.

Comparison of adjectives

1. Comparatives

più ... di	more ... than	**(tanto) ...quanto**	as ... as
meno ... di	less ... than	**(così) ... come**	as ... as

Daniela è più vecchia di Stefano.
Daniela is older than Stefano.

Firenze è (così) bella come Roma.
Florence is as beautiful as Rome.

Some regular and irregular comparative forms:

buono good; **più buono/migliore** better
cattivo bad; **più cattivo/peggiore** worse
grande big; **più grande/maggiore** bigger
piccolo small; **più piccolo/minore** smaller

2. Superlatives

il più / la più (the most) **il meno / la meno** (the least)

For: 'Florence is the most beautiful city' you can say:
Firenze è la più bella città or **Firenze è la città più bella.**

Some regular and irregular superlative forms:
il più buono/il migliore the best
il più cattivo/il peggiore the worst
il più grande/il maggiore the biggest
il più piccolo/il minore the smallest
Il maggiore vantaggio di Internet è ...
The biggest advantage of the Internet is ...

For "very ..." you can add **-issimo** to the adjective:
Pisa è bellissima. Pisa is very beautiful.

Some regular and irregular superlative forms:
buonissimo/ottimo very good
cattivissimo/pessimo very bad
grandissimo/massimo very big
piccolissimo/minimo very small

➜ Useful pages in *Amici*: 61, 212

aiuto !

When preparing for your Writing or Speaking tasks, try to use a variety of tenses, time expressions, vocabulary and adjectives. Adapt the sentences in this Chapter, e.g.

Marco è <u>più alto</u> di Daniela.

Roma è <u>la più bella</u> capitale d'Europa.

Il calcio è un gioco <u>interessantissimo</u>!

Home and Local Area

3.1 Special occasions celebrated in the home

Buon anno/Felice anno nuovo!	*Happy New Year!*
Buon Natale!	*Merry Christmas!*
Buona Pasqua!	*Happy Easter!*
Buon compleanno!	*Happy Birthday!*
Buon divertimento!	*Have a good time!*
Buone Feste!	*Enjoy the celebrations!*
Che bella sorpresa!	*What a lovely surprise!*
Che bello!	*How nice!*
Come sei gentile!	*How kind you are!*

brindare	*to toast*
celebrare/festeggiare	*to celebrate*
offrire un regalo	*to give a present*
passare	*to pass, spend*
regalare	*to give as a present*
ricevere	*to receive*
ringraziare	*to thank*

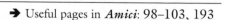

l'albero di Natale	*Christmas tree*
Babbo Natale	*Father Christmas*
la befana	*befana*
Capodanno	*New Year*
Epifania	*Epiphany*
Gesù Bambino	*baby Jesus*
la Messa	*Mass*
il panettone	*Italian Christmas cake*
il periodo natalizio	*Christmas period*
il presepe/presepio	*nativity scene*
Santo Stefano	*Saint Stephen, Boxing Day*
il veglione di Capodanno	*New Year's Eve party*
la Vigilia di Natale	*Christmas Eve*
il battesimo	*baptism, christening*
la prima comunione	*First Communion*
la cresima	*Confirmation*
la bomboniera	*bomboniera*
i confetti	*sugared almonds*
il compleanno	*birthday*
l'onomastico	*Saint's day, name day*
la tradizione	*tradition*
Carnevale	*Carnival time*
i coriandoli	*confetti*
Festa del papà	*Father's Day*
Festa della donna	*Women's Day*
Festa del Lavoro	*May Day, Labour Day*
Festa della Repubblica	*Republic Day, 2nd June*
Festa della mamma	*Mother's Day*

➜ Useful pages in *Amici*: 98–103, 193

1. ▭ Read Alessandro's account of Christmas Day and answer the
    following questions in English. **(H)**

Mi sono svegliato un po' più tardi del solito, oltre tutto con un gran mal
di testa che continua a persistere. Dovevamo andare al pranzo dai nonni,
ma visto che mamma non sta bene siamo rimasti a casa. Dopo pranzo è
arrivata la mia ragazza e ci siamo scambiati i regali e poi abbiamo fatto un
giochino stupido con il pc, poi c'erano parenti che andavano e venivano
quindi auguri qua, auguri là ... Adesso sono stanco morto e mi metterei
volentieri a dormire ... **Alessandro**

(a) When did Alessandro wake up?

(b) How was he feeling when he woke up?

(c) Whose house were they going to for lunch?

(d) Why did they not go?

(e) What did Alessandro and his girlfriend do after lunch?

(f) How does Alessandro feel now?

2. ∩ Listen to Daniela and Elena talking about Christmas (CD track 19)
    and complete the sentences in English. **(F)**

(a) Daniela has just written _____ .

(b) Daniela and Stefano used to look forward to
    _____ .

(c) They used to go to _____ .

(d) Their relations always had in their home
    _____ .

(e) On the table there were always _____ .

(f) Later they went to _____ .

3. ∩ Listen to this person talking about Christmas (CD track 20) and
    answer the following questions in English. **(H)**

(a) What did father bring home and when exactly did he bring it?

(b) On what date did they go to church and why would it have made
    sense to take the car?

(c) What did they find under the tree when they got home?
    (mention **two** items)

(d) When could they have a sweet from the tree?

(e) What had already happened before the Befana arrived?

3.2 Home town, neighbourhood and region, where it is and what it is like

Abito ...   *I live ...*

a Londra/Edimburgo   *in London/Edinburgh*
in Scozia/Galles   *in Scotland/Wales*
in Inghilterra/Irlanda   *in England/Ireland*
in un paese   *in a village*
in un quartiere residenziale   *in a residential area*
in periferia   *in the suburbs*
vicino al mare   *near the sea*
accanto allo stadio   *next to the stadium*
di fronte al cinema   *opposite the cinema*
lontano dalla città   *a long way from town*

(Non) c'è molto da fare   *There is (not) a lot to do*
C'è un castello   *There is a castle*
C'è una fattoria   *There is a farm*
Ci sono i fiori   *There are flowers*
Ci sono dei monumenti   *There are monuments*
Si può andare al cinema   *You can go to the cinema*

La mia casa si trova in periferia	*My house is in the suburbs*
Ha tre piani	*It has three floors*
Al primo piano ci sono due camere da letto	*On the first floor there are two bedrooms*
Abbiamo un giardino circondato da una siepe	*We have a garden surrounded by a hedge*
Abito in una casa a schiera	*I live in a terraced house*
Il tetto è rosso	*The roof is red*
Di fronte alla casa c'è un giardino	*There's a garden in front of the house*
Il giardino è recintato	*The garden is fenced*
Dietro all'appartamento c'è un garage	*Behind the flat there is a garage*
Di sopra ci sono due bagni	*There are two bathrooms upstairs*
Al pianterreno c'è una sala da pranzo	*On the ground floor there is a dining room*
Al primo piano c'è un salotto	*There is a lounge on the first floor*
Al secondo piano c'è una camera per gli ospiti	*There is a guest room on the second floor*
Non c'è ascensore	*There is no lift*
Ci sono le scale	*There are stairs*

➜ Useful pages in *Amici*: 30–35, 185

1. 📖 Read these comments about Pisa.

Pisa sa restare nel cuore della gente anche non pisana non solo per la sua Torre e la sua Piazza ... ma per tutto quello che di bello ed unico sa mostrare e non solo artisticamente ... Un bacione **Beatrice**

Ciao, io trovo Pisa una città bellissima, io ci studio, frequento la facoltà di Giurisprudenza ma comunque vivo a Torre del Lago Puccini. Da quando ho iniziato a studiare qui, voglio rimanerci sempre, anche quando l'università è chiusa e spesso infatti ci sono tornata con il mio ragazzo e ci siamo seduti in riva all'Arno ad ammirare il paesaggio e gli edifici storici riflessi sull'acqua. È una città intellettuale e carica di arte, mi piace moltissimo! Baci **Carla**

Bella Pisa, a me piace molto la zona intorno al fiume. Mi sarebbe piaciuto studiare a Pisa! Adoro le città toscane. Lo so che tra città toscane c'è molta rivalità, ma sono tutte molto belle per me che sono piemontese. Io e mia moglie spesso siamo tentati a cambiare lavoro e venire in Toscana. **Aldo**

Write **B** (Beatrice), **C** (Carla), **A** (Aldo), or **N** (no-one). **(F/H)**

(a) Who would like to have studied in Pisa? ☐

(b) Who does not like Pisa? ☐

(c) Who has sat by the river and admired the view? ☐

(d) Who has considered working in Tuscany? ☐

(e) Who thinks Pisa is artistically beautiful/unique? ☐

(f) Who has bought a house in Pisa? ☐

(g) Who studies Law in Pisa? ☐

2. 🎧 Listen to two people talking about their homes (CD track 21). Complete the details by crossing out the incorrect information. The first one has been done for you. **(F)**

		Person 1	Person 2
(a)	Location	~~Town~~/Suburbs	Town/Suburbs
(b)	Balcony	Yes/No	Yes/No
(c)	No. of floors	1/2/3/4/5/6	1/2/3/4/5/6
(d)	Garden	Yes/No	Yes/No

Environment

3.3 Current problems facing the planet

C'è l'inquinamento …	
del mare	*There is sea pollution*
del fiume	*There is river pollution*
dell'aria	*There is air pollution*
causato dal traffico	*There is traffic pollution*
C'è troppo inquinamento	*There is too much pollution*
C'è troppo rumore	*There is too much noise*
C'è troppo traffico	*There is too much traffic*
Ci sono troppe macchine	*There are too many cars*
L'industria causa molto inquinamento	*Industry causes a lot of pollution*
Le macchine inquinano l'aria	*Cars pollute the air*
L'aria è inquinata dalle macchine	*The air is polluted by the cars*
La nostra salute è minacciata dall'inquinamento	*Our health is threatened by pollution*
La nostra salute è stata minacciata dall'inquinamento	*Our health has been threatened by pollution*
L'effetto serra minaccia la nostra terra	*The greenhouse effect threatens our earth*
Non ci sono abbastanza parcheggi	*There are not enough car parks*
Non ci sono abbastanza parchi	*There are not enough parks*
Non ci sono abbastanza piste ciclabili	*There are not enough cycle tracks*
Non ci sono abbastanza spazi per lasciare le biciclette	*There are not enough spaces to leave cycles*
Non ci sono abbastanza zone pedonali	*There are not enough pedestrian areas*
Bisogna chiudere al traffico il centro storico	*The old part of the town should be closed to traffic*
L'effetto serra è causato dalla presenza nell'atmosfera di alcuni gas serra	*The greenhouse effect is caused by greenhouse gases in the atmosphere*
Il buco dell'ozono è causato dai cloro fluoro carburi (CFC)	*The hole in the ozone is caused by CFCs*

→ Useful pages in *Amici*: 146–147

1. ▢▢ Read the text on pollution and complete each sentence by choosing the correct word from the box. **(H)**

> L' inquinamento è un grave problema che la società d'oggi sta affrontando dal momento che le grandi compagnie commerciali, alimentari, petrolifere e le varie industrie compromettono l'ambiente modificando le nostre condizioni di vita.
>
> L'inquinamento può essere di vario genere, quello acustico è il più diffuso e può causare disturbi psico-fisici, stress e depressione. I più esposti sono gli operai, le casalinghe e i giovani. Una prolungata esposizione a rumori (aerei, elettrodomestici, da discoteche e concerti) può causare anche sordità.
>
> Un altro tipo d'inquinamento invisibile ma letale è causato dalle onde elettromagnetiche, emesse da cellulari, antenne, forni a microonde e strumenti di telecomunicazione. A lungo andare i cellulari possono causare tumori e forti mal di testa. I più esposti a questo rischio sono i giovani e i pendolari che molto spesso usano più di un cellulare.

(a) Pollution is a _____ problem.

(b) Many _____ companies and industries are damaging our environment.

(c) One of the most widespread types of pollution is _____ and among the most vulnerable are _____ . In the worst cases, this type of pollution can also cause _____ .

(d) Another type of pollution is caused by electromagnetic waves from _____ .

(e) Mobile phones can result in very bad _____ and those most at risk include _____ .

microwaves	headaches	earache	deafness	different
commuters	electric pylons	serious	housewives	unique
similar	the elderly	noise	blindness	litter

2. 🎧 Listen to Daniela talking about living near Florence (CD track 22). Is her attitude positive or negative? Write **P** (positive) or **N** (negative) in the table. **(F)**

(a)	The city of Florence	
(b)	The traffic	
(c)	Getting around on foot	
(d)	Pedestrian areas	
(e)	Living in Sesto Fiorentino	

3.4 Being environmentally friendly within the home and local area

Vogliamo salvare la natura	*We want to save nature*
Dobbiamo riusare ogni cosa	*We must re-use everything*
Porto i vecchi giornali nell'apposito contenitore	*I take old newspapers to the right container*
Riciclo i farmaci scaduti	*I recycle out of date medicines*
Porto le bottiglie di vetro nell'apposito contenitore	*I take glass bottles to the right container*
Bisogna riciclare i nostri rifiuti	*We must recycle our rubbish*
È essenziale risparmiare l'acqua di casa	*It's essential to save household water*
Bisogna usare di più i mezzi pubblici	*We must use public transport more*
È importante riusare i sacchetti di plastica	*It's important to re-use plastic bags*
È necessario risparmiare elettricità	*We should save electricity*
È importante scegliere confezioni biodegradabili	*It's important to choose biodegradable packaging*
È importante scegliere confezioni riciclabili	*It's important to choose recyclable packaging*
Non abbandonare i rifiuti nell'ambiente!	*Don't leave rubbish in the environment!*
Non accendere fuochi nei boschi!	*Don't light fires in the woods!*
Non buttare la gomma per terra!	*Don't throw chewing gum on the ground!*
Non fare troppo rumore!	*Don't make too much noise!*
Non scrivere graffiti!	*Don't write any graffiti!*
Risparmia l'acqua!	*Save water!*
Riusa più volte i sacchetti di plastica!	*Re-use plastic bags several times!*
Spegni le luci!	*Switch off lights!*
Usa di più i mezzi pubblici!	*Use public transport more!*
Usa meno la macchina!	*Use the car less!*
Il buco dell'ozono è causato dai cloro fluoro carburi (CFC)	*The hole in the ozone is caused by CFCs*

→ Useful pages in *Amici*: 148–151, 155, 199

1. ▭ Read this information about sorting your rubbish. **(F)**

- Cosa si può differenziare: giornali, riviste, quaderni, vecchi libri, carta pulita in generale.
- Cosa si può differenziare: bottiglie, barattoli, vasetti di qualsiasi colore (senza i tappi metallici).
- Cosa si può differenziare: lattine, scatolette, contenitori, fogli e vassoi di alluminio, tappi dei barattoli e delle bottiglie.
  Qualche consiglio pratico: schiacciate le lattine per ridurne il volume. I contenitori devono essere per quanto possibile puliti.
- Cosa si può differenziare: bottiglie d'acqua e di bibite, flaconi dei detersivi, dello shampoo e contenitori per liquidi in generale.
  Qualche consiglio pratico: Svuotate le bottiglie, schiacciatele lateralmente e richiudetele per evitare che riacquistino volume.
- Cosa si può differenziare: Avanzi di cibo, scarti di cucina, alimenti avariati, resti di frutta e verdura, foglie, rami e fiori delle piante.

Write the letter(s) of the words in the table alongside the appropriate container heading.

A	tin cans
B	jars
C	vegetable peelings
D	shampoo bottles
E	jar and bottle tops
F	magazines
G	food leftovers
H	exercise books

(a)	Carta e cartone	
(b)	Vetro	
(c)	Metalli	
(d)	Plastica	
(e)	Umido	

2. ◖ Listen to the following people talking about their actions (CD track 23). Match the action with the correct person. **(H)**

1	
2	
3	
4	
5	
6	
7	

A Throws leaflets on the ground.

B Always travels to work by car.

C Cycles everywhere.

D Wastes electricity.

E Doesn't take plastic bottles to a recycling centre.

F Recycles most household rubbish.

G Uses more water by taking a bath.

H Doesn't put anything in the recycling bins.

I Never takes a shopping bag to the supermarket.

A quick reminder:

The passive

The passive is formed when the object of the sentence becomes the subject. Compare these two sentences:

Le macchine inquinano l'aria. Cars pollute <u>the air</u>. (object)

L'aria è inquinata dalle macchine.
<u>The air</u> (subject) is polluted by cars. (passive)

In Italian the passive can be used in all tenses. You need the verb **essere** + the past participle of the verb. The past participle(s) must agree with the subject e.g.

present (minacciare)	future
è minacciato/a	sarà minacciato/a
sono minacciati/e	saranno minacciati/e
imperfect	**perfect**
era minacciato/a	è stato/a minacciato/a
erano minacciati/e	sono stati/e minacciati/e

La nostra salute <u>è</u> minacciata dall'inquinamento.
Our health <u>is</u> threatened by pollution.

La nostra salute <u>è stata</u> minacciata dall'inquinamento.
Our health <u>has been</u> threatened by pollution.

La nostra salute <u>era</u> minacciata dall'inquinamento.
Our health <u>was</u> threatened by pollution.

La nostra salute <u>sarà</u> minacciata dall'inquinamento.
Our health <u>will be</u> threatened by pollution.

You can avoid the passive in Italian by using:
* **si** + the third person singular/plural of the verb:
Si vedono graffiti dappertutto. Graffiti can be seen everywhere.
* the active form of the verb:
L'inquinamento minaccia la nostra salute.
Pollution is threatening our health.

Impersonal verbs

Impersonal verbs have the subject 'it' or 'there' not 'I, you' etc. Frequently used impersonal constructions start with **è**:

È essenziale/importante/necessario riciclare tutto.
It is essential/important/necessary to recycle everything.

È meglio usare i mezzi pubblici. It is better to use public transport.

A common impersonal verb is **bisogna (bisognare)** 'it is necessary' and it is only used in this form.

Bisogna riciclare i nostri rifiuti. It is necessary to recycle our rubbish.

→ Useful pages in *Amici*: 149, 150, 214–215, 219

Adapt some of the sentences in this Chapter to include the passive and/or impersonal verbs. Add some connectives.

La nostra salute è minacciata dall'inquinamento, perciò è importante aiutare l'ambiente.

Pronouns

subj.	reflex.	dir. object	ind. object	emphatic
io	mi	mi	mi	me
tu	ti	ti	ti	te
lui	si	lo	gli	lui
lei	si	la	le	lei
Lei	si	La	Le	Lei
noi	ci	ci	ci	noi
voi	vi	vi	vi	voi
loro	si	li	loro/gli	loro
Loro	si	Le	Loro/gli	Loro

Subject pronouns are only used for clarity or emphasis.
Io vado in bicicletta ma lui va in macchina.
I go by bike, but he goes by car.

Reflexive pronouns are used with reflexive verbs.
La mia casa si trova in periferia.
My house is situated on the outskirts.

Direct object pronouns are normally placed in front of the verb and agree with the noun they replace.
Vedi la zona pedonale? No, non la vedo.
Can you see the pedestrian zone? No, I can't see it.
Le piste ciclabili? Le ho già viste.
The cycle lanes? I have already seen them.

Indirect object pronouns are normally placed in front of the verb, but **loro** (often replaced by **gli** in modern Italian) always comes after the verb:
Le ho chiesto di spegnere la luce. I asked her to switch off the light.

With **dovere**, **potere**, **sapere**, **volere**, pronouns can be placed in front of the verb or after the infinitive:
Te lo posso mandare / Posso mandartelo. I can send it to you.

Emphatic pronouns are used with a preposition.
* for emphasis: **Questo regalo è per te.** This present is for you.
* when the verb has two or more direct or indirect objects:
Chiederò a lei non a lui. I shall ask her not him.
* as the second part of a comparison:
Sei più alto di me. You are taller than me.

Si is a reflexive pronoun meaning 'himself/herself/themselves' etc, but also 'one'. **Non si sa mai.** One never knows.

Ci to it/this/that, about it/this/that; here/there:
Pensaci! Think about it!

Ne 'of/about him/her/them/this; from here/there'.
Cosa ne pensate? What do you think about this?

Order of pronouns
When two pronouns are used, the indirect comes before the direct, or before **ne**.

Try to use some pronouns in your work e.g.
C'è troppa carta nella casa. Dovrei riciclarla.

➜ Useful pages in *Amici*: 81, 87, 220–222

School/College and Future Plans

4.1 What school/college is like

Frequento …	*I attend …*
Ci sono cinque lezioni al giorno	*There are five lessons a day*
Le lezioni cominciano alle 9	*Lessons start at 9.00*
Finiscono verso le 3.30	*They finish about 3.30*
C'è un intervallo di 10 minuti	*There is a 10 minute break*
C'è una pausa per il pranzo di … minuti	*There is a … minute lunch break*
Pranzo a mezzogiorno	*I have lunch at midday*
Mangio alla mensa	*I eat in the canteen*
Pranzo a casa	*I have my lunch at home*
Faccio 13 materie in tutto	*I do 13 subjects in all*
La mia materia preferita è …	*My favourite subject is …*
Detesto i compiti	*I hate homework*
Studio l'inglese, …	*I study English, …*
È possibile fare sport individuali e di squadra	*It's possible to do team and individual sports*

l'arte (f)	*art*	la letteratura	*literature*
la biologia	*biology*	la lettura	*reading*
la chimica	*chemistry*	la lezione	*lesson*
il disegno	*art*	la lingua	*language*
l'economia	*economics*	la matematica	*maths*
l'educazione fisica	*PE*	le lingue straniere	*foreign languages*
la fisica	*physics*	la materia	*subject*
il francese	*French*	la musica	*music*
la geografia	*geography*	la religione	*religion*
la ginnastica	*gymnastics*	il russo	*Russian*
il greco	*Greek*	le scienze	*science*
l'informatica	*ICT*	lo spagnolo	*Spanish*
l'inglese (m)	*English*	lo sport	*sport*
l'italiano	*Italian*	la storia	*history*
il latino	*Latin*	il tedesco	*German*

la biblioteca con i computer	*library with computers*
il laboratorio scientifico	*science laboratory*
il laboratorio informatico	*ICT room*
l'aula di musica insonorizzata	*sound-proof music room*
con collegamento a Internet	*with Internet access*
con impianto di proiezione	*with projection facilties*

➜ Useful pages in *Amici*: 42–46, 156–157, 187

1. ▢▢ Read Marco's description of his school. **(F/H)**

> **La nostra aula** è al primo piano della scuola. È un'aula molto spaziosa
> che dà sui campi sportivi. Il mio banco è accanto alla finestra e quindi
> se la lezione è noiosa posso guardare quelli che giocano a calcio o a
> pallacanestro. Nell'aula ci sono parecchi scaffali dove ci sono libri e
> quaderni di alunni e maestri ma purtroppo non abbiamo computer.
>
> **La biblioteca** è spaziosa e luminosa. Si trova al piano terra, proprio
> davanti all'ingresso. Lungo le pareti ci sono gli scaffali con i libri ed in
> un angolo c'è la scrivania dove il bibliotecario segna al computer i libri
> che prendiamo in prestito. La parete davanti all'entrata è tutta a vetri e c'è
> la porta per uscire in giardino. In biblioteca c'è sempre silenzio e ci vado
> spesso a fare i miei compiti.
>
> **L'aula di informatica** si trova al secondo piano ed è abbastanza ampia
> e luminosa. Nell'aula computer, appena si entra a destra, ci sono quattro
> computer, a sinistra invece ce ne sono sei. Davanti alla porta c'è una
> lavagna ed accanto alla lavagna ci sono delle grandi finestre.

Which of the following statements are **T** (true), **F** (false), **?** (not in the
text)?

(a) Marco's desk is next to the door. ▢

(b) He plays football during the break. ▢

(c) There is no space for books in the classroom. ▢

(d) The library is on the ground floor. ▢

(e) There are no computers in the library. ▢

(f) Marco often works in the library. ▢

(g) There is a door from the library into the garden. ▢

(h) The computer room is small and quite dark. ▢

(i) The computer room is also open after school. ▢

2. ◖◗ Listen to Stefano and Daniela talking about school (CD track 24)
and complete the following statements in English. **(F/H)**

(a) At school Stefano studies _____ .

(b) Stefano studies English _____ and has
lessons _____ a week.

(c) He decided to take English _____ .

(d) The English course Daniela describes lasts
_____ a year. The lessons last
_____ and they have one lesson
_____ .

4.2 Pressures and problems

arrabbiarsi	*to get annoyed*
il bullismo fisico/verbale	*physical/verbal bullying*
il bullo	*bully*
colpire con pugni o calci	*punch or kick*
i compiti	*homework*
comportamenti antisociali	*antisocial behaviour*
dare un esame	*to sit an examination*
difficile	*difficult*
dimenticare	*to forget*
l'esame (m)	*exam*
facile	*easy*
fare i compiti	*to do homework*
insultare	*to insult*
marinare la scuola	*to play truant*
passare un esame	*to pass an examination*
prendere un bel/brutto voto	*to get a good/bad mark*
il problema	*problem*
il risultato	*result*
severo	*strict*
lo studio	*study, studying*
il tema	*topic, theme, essay*
la vittima	*victim*
il voto	*mark*

Mi piacciono gli insegnanti, ma alcuni sono severi	*I like the teachers but some are strict*
Penso che l'insegnante abbia ragione	*I think that the teacher is right*
Penso che sia importante	*I think (that) it is important*
Secondo me, è importante	*In my opinion, it's important*

Gli esami sono estremamente importanti	*Exams are extremely important*
(Non) sono bravo nella maggior parte delle materie	*I am (not) good in most of the subjects*
Mi sento nervoso quando do/faccio gli esami scritti	*I feel nervous when I do written exams*
(Non) ho sempre avuto dei bei voti	*I have (not) always had good marks*
L'importanza dei risultati causa molto stress	*The importance of results causes a lot of stress*
Secondo me la ripetizione di un anno non è giusta	*In my opinion repeating a year is not a good thing*

➔ Useful pages in *Amici*: 158–159, 200

1. 📖 Read about Clara's problem and answer the following questions in English. **(F/H)**

> Ciao ragazzi, vorrei parlarvi di un mio problema con la scuola: frequento il quarto anno del liceo classico e ci sommergono letteralmente di compiti e ovviamente faccio parecchie materie che includono greco, chimica, letteratura inglese e filosofia tant'è che devo studiare circa sei o sette ore quasi ogni giorno. È vero che io sono particolarmente ansiosa perché ho paura di andare male. Il problema è che non riesco più a uscire durante la settimana oltre il sabato. Come se non bastasse i proff. fanno una sorta di terrorismo psicologico su noi alunni che non fa che accrescere il nostro stress. Sono sempre nervosa, stressata e non ho altri interessi oltre alla scuola e quando riesco a trovare un giorno libero mi sento in colpa se non studio! Sto cominciando a non farcela veramente più, se vedo un libro mi sento male, se penso alle interrogazioni ancora peggio. Vorrei cambiare scuola. Non so più che fare, la scuola sta diventando un vero e proprio problema per me! Che mi consigliate?
> **Clara**

(a) What type of school does Clara attend and which year is she in?

(b) What is her main complaint?

(c) Which subjects does she mention?

(d) What is her problem during the week?

(e) How does she feel when the teachers push her to do more work?

(f) Why does she feel guilty if she has a day off?

(g) How does she describe her feelings at the end of the message?

2. 🎧 Listen to these students talking about their teachers (CD track 25). **(F)**
Write if their attitude is **P** (positive), **N** (negative) or **P+N** (positive and negative). Give one reason to justify your answer.

	P/N	Reason
1		
2		
3		
4		
5		

Current and Future Jobs

4.3 Looking for and getting a job

Sono studente/ssa	*I am a student*
Sono disoccupato/a	*I am unemployed*
Mio padre è ingegnere	*My father is an engineer*
Mia madre è dottoressa	*My mother is a doctor*
Lavoro in un albergo	*I work in a hotel*
Lavora in una banca	*He works in a bank*
Lavoro per una società che si chiama …	*I work for a company called …*
Lavoro come infermiera	*I work as a nurse*
Io ho lavorato nei mesi estivi in un ufficio	*I worked in an office in the summer months*
L'anno scorso ho lavorato come cameriere/a	*Last year I worked as a waiter/ waitress*
Durante l'estate ho lavorato in un ristorante	*During the summer I worked in a restaurant*
Ho fatto un corso di informatica	*I have done an ICT course*
Mi piacerebbe viaggiare	*I would like to travel*
Mi piacerebbe tanto lavorare presso …	*I'd very much like to work at …*
Vorrei andare in Australia	*I'd like to go to Australia*
Vorrei diventare autista	*I'd like to be a driver*
Vorrei diventare giornalista	*I'd like to be a journalist*
Vorrei lavorare a tempo pieno	*I'd like to work full time*
Vorrei lavorare con gli animali	*I'd like to work with animals.*
Vorrei lavorare con i computer	*I'd like to work with computers*
Vorrei lavorare in un albergo/ ristorante	*I'd like to work in a hotel/ restaurant*
Vorrei studiare scienze all'università	*I would like to study science at university*
Desidero vivere in Italia	*I would like to live in Italy*
Ho intenzione di lavorare come traduttore/traduttrice	*I intend to work as a translator*
Ho un'ottima conoscenza dell'inglese scritto	*I have excellent written English*
Ho un'ottima conoscenza di Internet	*I have an excellent knowledge of the Internet*
Lavoro volentieri in un team	*I like to work in a team*
Spero di fare l'interprete	*I hope to be an interpreter*
Vorrei migliorare la mia conoscenza dell'italiano	*I would like to improve my Italian*

➜ Useful pages in *Amici*: 112–115, 195

1. ☐☐ Read the following job adverts and then match up the right person for the job. Write the correct letter in the boxes. **(F/H)**

A Cercasi commessa/o esperta/o part-time per negozio calzature in Sesto Fiorentino. Inviare curriculum con autorizzazione al trattamento dei dati personali.

B Cerchiamo per tutte le città italiane persone serie e motivate per aprire nuova redazione di un quotidiano on line a network nazionale.

C Lavoro da casa con Internet, indipendente ed autonomo, sia part-time che full-time, senza alcun obbligo di orari. Se pensi di essere una persona dinamica con: grande determinazione, ottime capacità relazionali, intraprendenza e volontà di lavorare in autonomia, allora la nostra attività online da casa potrebbe fare per te.

D Agenti rappresentanti per vendita olio e vino in tutta Italia ed estero.

E Studio legale con sede a Berlino (Germania) cerca giovane avvocato (ambosessi) con buone conoscenze della lingua tedesca/inglese. Ottime prospettive di carriera.

F Cerco cuoco per ristorante a pranzo e cena con esperienza lavorativa, veloce nella preparazione e organizzazione del servizio, serio, disponibile a effettuare servizi di catering in caso di necessità.

(a) John has done a high level wine tasting course and would like to work as a salesman abroad. ☐

(b) Mary studied journalism at university. She speaks Italian and is highly motivated. ☐

(c) Susan already works as a solicitor, is career-minded and speaks fluent French and German. ☐

(d) Mark is an experienced sales assistant. He has worked in several different shops and also had a job in Italy. ☐

(e) Julia would like to spend more time with her children and wants a job where she can work from home. ☐

2. 🎧 Listen to these people talking about their work (CD track 26) and complete the table. **(F)**

	Person	Occupation	Opinion
(a)	Alessandro		
(b)	Giulia		
(c)	Gianluca		
(d)	Annamaria		
(e)	Isabella		

4.4 Advantages and disadvantages of different jobs

Mi piace il lavoro	*I like the job*
Mi piace tantissimo il mio lavoro	*I really like my job*
Il lavoro è interessante	*The job is interesting*
Non è un lavoro noioso	*It's not a boring job*
Comincio alle … Finisco alle …	*I start at … I finish at …*
L'orario è flessibile	*The hours are flexible*
Non devo lavorare il sabato	*I don't have to work on Saturdays*
Viaggio spesso	*I often travel*
Mi piace visitare altri Paesi	*I like to visit other countries*
Mi piace lavorare con i giovani	*I like working with young people*
Mi piaceva soprattutto incontrare i turisti	*Above all I liked meeting the tourists*
Alcuni turisti erano molto simpatici	*Some tourists were very nice*
Mi hanno pagato bene	*They paid me well*
Mi piaceva molto il lavoro	*I really liked the job*
Mi piacerebbe diventare sia attore che cantante rock	*I'd like to be an actor or a rock singer*
Mi piacerebbe diventare un giocatore di basket	*I'd like to become a basketball player*
Le piace il suo lavoro Gli piace il suo lavoro	*She likes her job* *He likes his job*

Il mio lavoro ha degli svantaggi	*My job has disadvantages*
È un lavoro duro	*It's a hard job*
Devo lavorare spesso a casa la sera	*I often have to work at home in the evening*
Questo è un vero svantaggio	*This is a real disadvantage*
Le ore lavorative sono lunghe	*The working hours are long*
Il lavoro è faticoso	*The job is tiring*
La paga è troppo bassa.	*The pay is too low*
Alcuni colleghi sono piuttosto antipatici	*Some colleagues are not very nice*
Non vado d'accordo con …	*I do not get on with …*
Non gli piace il suo lavoro Non le piace il suo lavoro	*He does not like his job* *She does not like her job*

➜ Useful pages in *Amici*: 112–115, 168, 195

1. ⬚ Read about the advantages and disadvantages of working from home and answer the following questions. **(H)**

<table>
<tr><td>

I VANTAGGI DEL TELELAVORO

I vantaggi per i lavoratori
- Grande flessibilità di orario (lavorare nelle ore in cui ci si sente più in forma)
- Necessità ridotta di spostamenti
- Risparmio delle spese
- Riduzione dello stress

I vantaggi per il datore di lavoro
- Maggiore flessibilità d'impiego dei dipendenti
- Retribuzione basata sul lavoro effettivamente svolto
- Taglio delle spese per la gestione di uffici

I vantaggi per la città
- Riduzione del traffico e dell'inquinamento nei centri cittadini

</td><td>

GLI SVANTAGGI DEL TELELAVORO

Ci sono tuttavia alcuni svantaggi.
- Molti si troverebbero all'improvviso senza lavoro (gli operai che producono i mezzi di trasporto, quelli che ne curano la manutenzione, gli autisti, i benzinai e via dicendo)
- Mancanza di contatto umano con i propri colleghi
- Problemi con la tecnologia
- Costi per attrezzature, hardware, software

</td></tr>
</table>

(a) Give **three** advantages of working from home.
(b) Give **two** advantages for the employer.
(c) What will be the positive outcome for the environment?
(d) Who might suffer from unemployment as a result?
(e) Give **two** problems people who work from home might face.

2. 🎧 Listen to Sandro talking about his job (CD track 27) and complete the sentences. **(F)**

(a) Sandro is a _____ .
(b) At the moment he works _____ .
(c) He is _____ with his job.
(d) Two disadvantages of working at night is that he rarely sees _____ and cannot go out with _____ .
(e) He has been doing this job for _____ .
(f) The _____ is good.
(g) Sometimes he works _____ a week.

1 Lifestyle

Health

1.1 Healthy and unhealthy lifestyles and their consequences

1(a) P+N; (b) N; (c) P; (d) N
2(a) Cycling and jogging;
  (b) Read lots of books
  (c) Fruit and vegetables
  (d) Fish
3(a) Didn't want to do any sport
  (b) Her boyfriend because she goes with him to the gym
  (c) Aerobics twice a week and water polo once a week
  (d) Bread and biscuits
  (e) A glass of water with lemon
  (f) Now she only tries healthy things

Relationships and Choices

1.2 Relationships with family and friends

1(a) F; (b) M+F; (c) N; (d) M; (e) N; (f) F
2(a) Simonetta
  (b) 19
  (c) Three brothers, one sister
  (d) Venezuela
  (e) Nice and amusing
3(a) D; (b) F; (c) H; (d) B; (e) I; (f) C

1.3 Future plans regarding marriage/partnership

1(a) T; (b) F; (c) ?; (d) T; (e) ?; (f) F; (g) F
2(a) Between 28 and 30
  (b) Go to university and then find a job
  (c) Tall, good looking and nice
  (d) She wouldn't want more than two, one boy and one girl if possible

1.4 Social Issues and Equality

1(a) 6.8; (b) (more than) 72; (c) 11.8 (d) 7.5; (e) 20
2(a) 17; (b) a month; (c) four years; (d) difficult; (e) a packet a day
3(a) Tell all his friends
  (b) Friends who were non-smokers because they didn't encourage him to smoke
  (c) Sweets because he had to chew something
  (d) He could play football much better
  (e) He didn't have money for anything else when he was smoking

2 Leisure

Free Time and the Media

2.1 Free time activities

1(a) F; (b) F; (c) M; (d) S; (e) F

2

(a)	playing tennis	in the park	a friend
(b)		cultural centre	friends
(c)	watching a football match		Stefano
(d)	going for a walk		friends
(e)	dancing	discotheque	
(f)			friend

3
Dialogue 1
  (a) About a crazy teacher/about a teacher who did silly/crazy things
  (b) It made her laugh, which she needed after a stressful day at work/in the office
Dialogue 2
  (a) The actors were very good
  (b) The plot was too complicated/ didn't understand anything/too long

2.2 Shopping, money, fashion and trends

1(a) B; (b) S; (c) E; (d) L; (e) F; (f) E; (g) B
2(a) shirt; (b) 40; (c) light blue; (d) dark blue; (e) 30 euro
3(a) 32 years, with her husband
  (b) Yes, they have fewer customers
  (c) Working mothers, open until late, you can get everything you need in the same shop
  (d) Negative outcomes are that lots of smaller shops have had to close and unemployment has increased. On the positive side the supermarket has given work to young people.

2.3 Advantages and disadvantages of new technology

1(a) Send messages/book plane or train tickets/shop without leaving your home
  (b) You can work from home and it's less expensive

(c) You can find out the weather forecast and the distance of your hotel from the airport

(d) The elderly, as they don't always know how to use it

(e) Back and eyesight problems

2(a) popular/United States

(b) interest

(c) 30%/Germany

(d) 40%/Sweden

(e) 230

3(a) You can discuss any topic and exchange all sorts of information with friends, colleagues and strangers

(b) People might find love/their soulmate

(c) He adopts a negative stance because we often don't know who we are communicating with

2.4 Plans, preferences, experiences

1(a) C; (b) B; (c) A; (d) C; (e) A; (f) C

2(a) Austria; (b) parents; (c) July 5th (d) ten days; (e) car; (f) had a good time

3(a) A; (b) C; (c) B; (d) B

2.5 What to see and getting around

1(a) T; (b) F; (c) ?; (d) F; (e) T; (f) T; (g) ?; (h) F

2(a) 2.00 am/two in the morning

(b) winter

(c) taxi

(d) apartment/flat

(e) penguins, koalas and kangaroos

(f) 100 kilometres

3(a) You can have a bicycle for free

(b) That they go for a ride

(c) Negative, because it's too hot

(d) By saying that it is cooler in the woods and it's only for an hour

(e) That they are joined by Marco and Daniela and they only go for an hour

3 Home and Environment

Home and Local Area

3.1 Special occasions celebrated in the home

1(a) Later than usual

(b) He had a really bad headache

(c) The grandparents' house

(d) The mother was ill and they stayed at home

(e) They exchanged presents and played a stupid game on the computer

(f) Very tired, wants to go to bed

2(a) an article for Gianpaolo

(b) Christmas

(c) their grandparents' home

(d) a Christmas tree decorated with lights

(e) sweets/fruit/meat

(f) Midnight Mass/church

3(a) A small Christmas tree; a few days before Christmas

(b) On 24 December; the church was a long way to walk

(c) Some small presents; a pair of gloves, a scarf, woollen socks

(d) Before going to bed and for the days following Christmas

(e) Usually all the sweets from the tree had been eaten

3.2 Home town, neighbourhood and region, where it is and what it is like

1(a) A; (b) N; (c) C; (d) A; (e) B; (f) N; (g) C

2(a) suburbs   town

(b) yes   yes

(c) two   five

(d) yes   yes

3.3 Current problems facing the planet

1(a) serious

(b) different

(c) noise/the elderly/deafness

(d) microwaves

(e) headaches/commuters

2(a) P; (b) N; (c) N; (d) P; (e) P

3.4 Being environmentally friendly within the home and local area

1(a) F, H; (b) B; (c) A, E; (d) D; (e) C, G

2 1 D; 2 H; 3 A; 4 G; 5 E; 6 I; 7 B

4 Work and education

School/College and Future Plans

4.1 What school/college is like

1 (a) F; (b) ?; (c) F; (d) T; (e) F; (f) T; (g) T; (h) F; (i) ?

2 (a) French and German
  (b) after school /twice
  (c) because it is an important language
  (d) 30 hours; one and a half hours; a week

4.2 Pressures and problems

1 (a) Secondary/grammar school; year 4
  (b) Too much homework
  (c) Greek, Chemistry, English literature, Philosophy
  (d) She can't go out any more (except on Saturdays)
  (e) She is nervous and stressed
  (f) She feels she should be studying
  (g) She feels ill if she sees a book/if she thinks about oral tests in class/she would like to change school

2 1 P; They are nice/intelligent.
   2 N; They are awful/elderly/fat/selfish.
   3 P+N; Sometimes they are severe, other times nice.
   4 N; They are severe.
   5 P; The teacher is calm.

Current and Future Jobs

4.3 Looking for and getting a job

1 (a) D; (b) B; (c) E; (d) A; (e) C

2 (a) Alessandro/doctor/interesting
  (b) Giulia/unemployed/boring
  (c) Gianluca/office worker/entertaining
  (d) Annamaria/nurse/difficult but satisfying
  (e) Isabella/housewife/tiring/hard

4.4 Advantages and disadvantages of different jobs

1 (a) Flexible working hours/less travelling/less expense/reduces stress
  (b) Can use his employees more flexibly/payment based on actual work done/cuts down on office expenditure
  (c) Reduction of traffic and pollution in the city centres
  (d) Workers who produce cars/buses etc., maintenance workers, drivers/service station attendants
  (e) No contact with colleagues/problems with IT/costs of buying hardware/software

2 (a) doctor
  (b) shifts
  (c) happy/satisfied
  (d) his two children ... his wife
  (e) ten years
  (f) pay
  (g) 60 hours

Tracklisting

MOUN
ROUTE GUIDE

YORKSHIRE DALES
& HOWGILL FELLS

Tim Woodcock

Dalesman

Dalesman Publishing Company
Stable Courtyard, Broughton Hall,
Skipton, North Yorkshire BD23 3AE

Text and photographs © Tim Woodcock, 1999

Route maps based upon the Ordnance Survey mapping with the
permission of The Controller of Her Majesty's Stationery Office
© Crown copyright (43462U)

Front cover: Descent of Buckden Pike; Back cover: Dentdale with
the Howgills beyond. Tim Woodcock

Locator map by Jeremy Ashcroft

A British Library Cataloguing in Publication record
is available for this book

ISBN 1 85568 150 1

Printed by Midas Printing (HK) Ltd

Slick-rock singletrack on Twistleton Scars (Route 21) page 82

DEDICATION

For Kay, the Boys and everyone at Appletreewick

AUTHOR'S ACKNOWLEDGEMENTS

Thanks first to the Dales Trail Guru, John Pitchers, for putting together
the initial selection of routes — which he and his friends have been
exploring for many years. Without his efforts this book would not have
been possible. Also to the Officers of the Yorkshire Dales National Park
for their advice and consideration and to Bolton Abbey Estate for
allowing cycling access through the Wharfe valley.

CONTENTS

THE RIDES

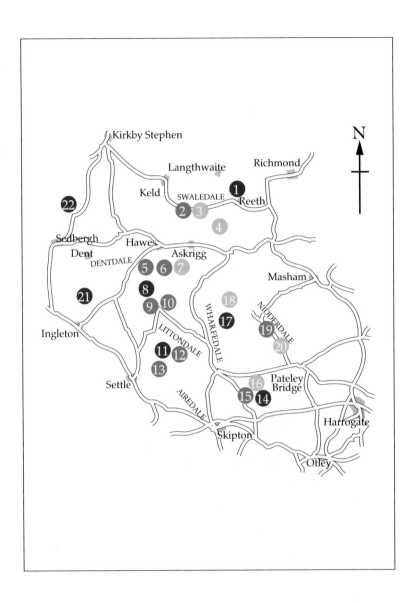

INTRODUCTION

The Yorkshire Dales and Howgill Fells offer one of the best mountain biking venues in the UK. There's no other area that can boast such a concentration of off-road routes suited to all abilities and there's no other place in England with such sublime scenery. Uniquely intimate dales, scattered with solitary barns and hemmed in by heather moor. Stark stone pavements, grit-stone crags and river-cut ravines. The scenery is ever-changing, beautiful and makes for exhilarating biking.

If you're a fat-tyre fanatic aching to etch an adrenaline-induced grin on your face then the legendary terrain of the Howgill Fells is the place to head for. A dramatic miniature massif squeezed in between the Pennine Ridge and Cumbrian Mountains, with precipitous pathways set to pitch any MTBer's mind over their matter. But if you don't want to put your heart where your mouth is then, to ensure a total contrast, seek out the sylvan beauty of Swaledale where ancient cart tracks keep the Swale company as it meanders east to Richmond. Between these two extremes are all types of terrain just waiting to feel your tyre imprint and implant a sense of wonder at your good fortune to be enjoying such an accessible sport in stunning surroundings. An ancient Roman road driving across Dodd Fell's sombre ridge; Wharfedale's shade-dappled pathways flicking between the trees; twisting, technical singletrack barrelling down Bowderdale's dun-coloured valley; spectacular winter sunsets seen from the high-flying tracks of Brant Fell; the wind-ruffled surface of Semer Water reflecting summer sun; the Arctic bleakness of the Whernsides in winter...... All of this and more are just waiting for you and your wheels to explore!

Twenty two fantastic rides. All of them have been planned with local mountain bikers and then ridden by the author. That wealth of local trail knowledge ensures that wherever you decide to take your wheels and test your trail skills you're going to experience the very best off-road routes the Dales have to offer.

Tim Woodcock
April 1999

PLANNING YOUR DAY

The routes

The routes described in this book are half-day and one day circular tours for off-road cyclists of all abilities. Of necessity 'day' is a very broad generalisation as time of year, weather, ground conditions and the rider's abilities will determine actual ride time.

Times

The time given for each route is based on the assumption that the riders are attempting a route matched to their capabilities and there are no prolonged stops. If you are mixing two routes or just riding part of a route you can calculate ride times quite accurately; assume an average speed of about 3-4mph in winter and 6-8mph in summer with a penalty of 1-2mph if the weather or ground conditions are bad. By habitually taking note of your estimated performance by comparison with your actual ride time you will soon get a good idea of how long your real 'day ride' can be.

Distance and height-gain

Rides of 20 miles or less can usually be slotted into a day with ease but rides of 30 miles and over need more careful scheduling. Although the length of each ride is an important factor don't be a slave to mileage. For the mountain biker height-gain is probably the most important, single determinant in the effort expended during a ride. As a rule of thumb rides making more than an average climb-rate of 1000ft/10 miles (300m/16km) will be strenuous – you need to be fit to really enjoy it! A day with more than 3500ft (1000m) of height-gain is going to be tough, especially in winter when daylight hours are few.

Grades

Each route has been given a grading according to its combined technical and physical demands:

FUN Low/moderate technical demands; not strenuous; ideal beginner's route or winter rides when the weather is bad.

SPORT Moderate technical demands; some hard cycling may be involved; ideal for those with some off-road experience or a 'quickie' for the fit.

EXPERT Difficult/severe technical sections; strenuous riding; for the fit and experienced rider.

These grades are subjective and are relevant only to the routes in this book.

Maps

This guide book comes complete with OS maps and detailed instructions. If you want to explore the Dales further the relevant Ordnance Survey

PLANNING

1:25000 Outdoor Leisure maps are No 2 Yorkshire Dales West; No 30 Yorkshire Dales Northern & Central; No 19 The Howgill Fells. The 1in Touring Map and Guide No 6 Yorkshire Dales gives a useful overview to the whole area. OS Outdoor Leisure 1:25000 scale maps covering most of the routes are available laminated; this makes them less of a handful when it's windy. To protect this book on the trail carry it in an A5-size clear plastic, zipped document case and use a book-mark to tag the route you're on. Always carry a map folded to show the terrain you are crossing.

Hardware

I could wax lyrical on the benefits of lightweight titanium frames, tell you suspension is a must and how SPDs are essential for smooth power transfer. Then tell you how to remortgage the house to finance the purchasing of that 'must have everything' trick bit and frameset. But I won't. To begin with, bike choice is a personal thing, fads and fashions change on a whim, and providing it's sound, any clunker of an MTB will do. Plus once you've remortgaged the house what do you do for the ultimate upgrade machine? Having said that there are some pointers as to what makes a bike well suited to the task and what does not.

Use a good quality, reasonably light, proper MTB – 21 or more indexed gears – with alloy wheels, low gearing and a comfortable saddle. You're looking for a bike built for comfort, not speed; one with a relatively upright position so look for a medium length, high-rise stem, wide handlebars and it's worth fitting bar-ends as they allow the rider to adopt a number of different riding positions. We're talking several hundred pounds here but if you're serious about mountain biking it's worth it. Take a look at the mountain biking press for what's what then ask at a good mountain bike shop and buy the best that you can afford. If that's out of your budget then consider hiring one; there are plenty of hire outlets in the Dales. Hiring is also a good way of 'balancing out' the hardware within a group. This is especially important if, for example, one of you has a clunker and the rest are riding lightweight titanium trickery decked out with suspension. A day-long 'megga' route will amplify the difference in ride quality, perhaps putting a downer on the whole outing. You should check your bike over before every ride, making sure it's fit to tackle the trails. Re-adjusting badly aligned brakes out on an exposed hillside, in winter, in the wet, is a pain but a block slipping into the spokes could spell disaster! It's also worth having your machine serviced by a qualified mechanic at regular intervals.

Dales trails can be pretty bumpy so there are some bike accessories that will make your off-road excursions more enjoyable: some branded, good quality treads, with around a 2in carcass of new rubber for cushioning and grip – consult a good MTB bike shop for what's the latest trend in tyres and avoid cheap 'imitations' as they're usually made with low-grade compound and won't grip so well; on this terrain there's also a case for some sort of cushioning to negate the effects of riding cobbly cart track – proper suspension is ideal but one of the many forms of 'flex-stem' coupled with a suspension seatpost works well.

Software

We're all aware of the weather's profound effect on our well-being – in the wet it's doom and gloom but once the sun pops out life's a party. It's all down to environment quality and it is clothing that determines the quality of our immediate environment – except that clothing choice is not decided on a whim of Nature. Kit yourself out with inappropriate gear that's been moth-balled in the wardrobe for the past five years and you're dressing up for a dose of doom and gloom. Uncomfortable. Take some time in selecting good quality kit and you'll be pleased to face whatever the weather throws at you.

Even in summer controlling warmth is the vital element, versatility the name of the game. Up on Buckden Pike it's normally a lot colder than down in Wharfedale. You can be shivering in the icy blast of a savage hailstorm while bikers down in the dale are still enjoying a summer's idyll.

Dress sense

Kitting out a mountain biker has proved to be one of the outdoor clothes designer's biggest challenges. It's a strenuous sport, generates loads of heat at peak activity then the loonies stand about mending punctures on a hill-side with a wind-chill factor of -10°C and their body temperature plummets faster than share prices on Black Monday. But designers are rising to the challenge and there's a stack of really good, MTB-specific gear to choose from.

The multi-layer principle is bandied about as the way to go – and it works – but there's always someone who has to swim against the tide and now there are several manufacturers producing single-layer, pile-lined kit. This is really late winter wear but can prove ideal for weight-saving freaks and experienced bikers out for a foul weather foray. So right from the start we're faced with a bewildering choice of kit, complicated by contrasting design convictions and all so technical that you need a science degree to discern what's what.

The best approach is to decide what you want the clothing to do. Ideally it should be light, have low bulk, be quick drying, resist the rampant sock syndrome, be easy to care for, fit well, feel comfortable and perform well – whether it's to provide warmth, windproofing or water-resistance (unless you're a fair-weather cyclist you'll need clothing to perform all of these functions). Above all it has to wick – let your body lose moisture and 'breathe'. Under-layer clothing that soaks up water, sags like a wet flannel and dims the lights when the tumble dryer is turned on is useless. Likewise, a top-layer that's built like a tent, flies like a kite and gives you your very own greenhouse effect is best left at home and used as a bin-liner. MTB and out-door magazines regularly review cycling kit, back-issues are easily obtainable – and their advice should at least put you on the right track.

Padded biking shorts are a must. There's no other item of clothing that will do so much for so little. Cut and style vary enormously and price does not necessarily reflect comfort and quality but generally the more panels they have the better, a seamless pad is less likely to chafe and for summer biking loose fit, touring shorts will keep you cooler. Female MTBers will find women's shorts far more comfortable than the equivalent man's version. Some folk are quite happy to bike without gloves but I invariably wipe out and grit my palms when I forget to put a pair on. Apart from protection for the accident-prone, padded mitts or gloves promote hands-on comfort levels, cushioning trail shock that may bruise you to your bones. On your feet there's nothing to beat a good pair of MTB boots. That's boots, not shoes. If you have SPDs check that your shoes have a deep, aggressive tread and that the cleats don't stand proud of the sole. (Pirouetting on a boulder on protruding cleats with a bike on your back isn't as funny as it looks!) Some SPDs also suffer from clogging when it gets really gloopy. And it can get seriously gloopy on some of the routes! There are alternatives to the ubiquitous SPD shoe such as light walking boots, mountaineering boots and even fell-running shoes with modified soles. They grip well and give ankle support. Don't be tempted by making do with trainers unless you're good at grass skiing with a bike on your back. Even a modest grass bank can be insurmountable if your boots sport an inadequate sole.

Last, but definitely not least, wear a helmet! I'm not going to tread lightly round this recommendation for fear of upsetting MTBers who want to express some notion of freedom by going bare-headed. One day you'll crack your nut and like as not it'll result in a call-out for the mountain rescue team; they'll not be pleased to find you weren't wearing a skid-lid.

If you're riding in cold, wet weather then you'll need to add extra clothing, especially thermals (tights, tops and socks), full gloves, headband/snood and waterproof socks. In winter an extra-warm fleece/windproof top, for when you're caught in the open with an emergency repair, lined mitts and lined hood will also be necessary if you're tackling the high level routes. On the hardware side don't forget lights – all it needs is a couple of punctures and before you know it the evening has closed in!

Navigation

Your mapping is in this book. Add a good quality compass on a neck cord and a weatherproof cycle computer – both of which you must be able to use with ease – and that's the pilot part sorted.

Survival kit

Mountain biking can be dangerous; a trivial accident above Cautley Spout or a major fall on Fountains Fell can quickly bring you down to a survival situation. A matter of life or death. Given the right kit, make the right decisions and you can turn crisis to drama, live to tell the tale and even laugh about it. Later. A good first aid kit and the knowledge to use it are essential. A basic kit should include antiseptic wipes, plasters, cohesive tape for wounds, triangular bandage, salt tablets for cramp and first aid instructions. (First aid information, covering some of the common MTB emergencies, is given on pages 18-21.) You might very well be an accomplished first-aider. Whoever comes to your aid might not and they, not to mention you, will appreciate a set of instructions ready to hand. Survival gear – mini-torch, survival bag and whistle – can all be packed with the first aid kit. Pack it in a heavy-duty, zip-tie polythene bag.

Tools and spares

Quality doesn't come cheap but good tools are a godsend when you're in a fix so be prepared to pay for them. Most multi-tools will save weight on a tool-roll of separate bits but don't forget to check that your clever widget does all the whatsits on your bike.

TOOL KIT	Pump
	Tyre levers
	Full set of Allen keys
	Small, adjustable wrench
	Screwdriver (cross-head and flat)
	Chain-splitter
	Spoke key
BIKE SPARES	Inner tube
	Puncture repair kit
	Brake blocks
	Cable ties
TRAIL KIT	Compass
	Computer
	First aid kit
	Survival kit (*whistle, bag, torch*)
	Emergency food (*cereal bars etc.*)
	Seat pack, bar or bum bag
	(*to keep emergency kit separated*)

Once you've got all tools and spares together pack them tight and keep them handy – ready for the inevitable trail-side emergency.

Bag it

Fell walkers are a common sight on the trail as popular walking and biking routes regularly coincide – and many of them will be strolling along with pint-sized day-packs to take their kit. Take a leaf out of their book. Travel light – use a bum-bag or, on more adventurous winter outings, a small ruck-sack – about 20 litres capacity.

FELL RIDING

RIDE SAFE. RIDE LIGHT. Mountain bikers have run the gauntlet of being alienated by other countryside users since the word go but the sport of mountain biking is flourishing. Road improvements have dramatically shrunk the distance separating metropolis from isolated moor and mountain so our wilderness areas have witnessed a motorised invasion of leisure seekers. For a time hikers (and to a lesser extent hackers) had it pretty much to themselves but today many people have found that cycling intensifies their enjoyment of the countryside. A rump of ramblers see us as rivals, ill-informed environmentalists call us erosionists and farmers fear speeding bikes will frighten stock and uncaring cyclists will flatten crops.

The fact that it's a re-run of early rambler versus landowner conflicts makes no difference. Neither does the fact that the hoary old chestnut 'cycle tyres cause serious erosion' is a proven misconception of some of our countryside companions. But we're here to stay and entrenched attitudes are already changing and this will come about more quickly if we ride responsibly.

Rights of way

Although we've taken every care to try and ensure that the routes described in this book will keep your cycling within the law, at the very least the status of some sections will change. (Details of path changes are published in an annual leaflet *Path Changes* available from the YDNP). Write to them, enclosing an sae, to the address on page 92). Plus, of course, you may get lost so it is as well to be sure of your rights of way.

Off-road cycling is permitted on bridleways, roads used as public paths (RUPPs), byways open to all traffic (BOATs), unclassified county roads (Greenways) and designated cycle paths. Some sections of some routes are open to us with the landowner's consent and this permissive access may be revoked at any time. Cycling is not permitted on footpaths, open land or on pavements. Do not rely on signposts as reliable indicators of a route's status – local authorities do not always make correct use of bridleway (Blue) and footpath (Yellow) waymarkers. If in doubt dismount. And remember, all land is owned by someone – even the remote moorland areas above the Dales – and you must take care not to trespass. If a landowner asks that you leave it is in your best interests, no matter what the right and wrong of it may be, to acquiesce.

Of course you may be bowling along a bridleway when up pops a barbed wire fence and the way is barred. It's a tricky situation because your rights are wrapped in a woolly bit of rhetoric which says you can remove the obstacle sufficiently to get past if it is reasonably possible or make a short detour to get round it. The landowner can demand recompense if you cause any damage so clambering over it – often the instinctive reaction – is not a clever thing to do. This doesn't happen often but Rights of Way across farmland do get blocked, ploughed up, are over-planted or are stocked with dangerous animals. Farmers are supposed to provide signed, alternative routes but if you're in doubt don't traipse across regardless. Check with the owner and if you're still forced off the Right of Way report it to the local authority – normally the Yorkshire Dales National Park – who will take up the matter on your behalf.

Codes of conduct

You won't be the first to ride these routes so you will be treading in the tyre tracks of others. If they've careered along, forged furrows across fields, stampeded livestock, left gates gaping and created a trail of havoc and mayhem then you're not going to get a warm reception from the countryside community. Nor is anybody else who follows along unless you follow the Country and Off-road Codes:

- Enjoy the countryside and respect its life and work
- Guard against all risk of fire
- Fasten all gates
- Keep dogs under control
- Keep to Public Rights of Way across farmland
- Use gates and stiles to cross boundaries
- Leave livestock, crops and machinery alone
- Take your litter home
- Do not contaminate water
- Protect wild flora and fauna
- Take special care on country roads
- Make no unnecessary noise
- Cycle only on permitted Rights of Way
- Give way to horse riders and walkers
- Do not ride in such a manner that you are a danger to others
- Do not race
- Keep erosion to a minimum and do not skid
- Be courteous and considerate to others
- Be self-sufficient and make sure your bike is safe to ride
- Wear a helmet
- Follow a route marked on a map
- Follow the Country Code

They're not really a set of rules so much as guides that any responsible, thoughtful member of the mountain biking community would adopt without a second thought.

RIDE SAFETY

Three's company – better than two – but four's an ideal number outdoors in the wilds. With a party of three, when one gets badly hurt, one can go for help and the third can stay with the casualty. But ideally two should go for help, not one, which is why four is better. More than four and mountain bikers in a bunch can be an intimidating party on a narrow path.

Abilities, strength and stamina in any group will vary. Keep within the capacity of everyone, watch your pace and make sure everyone keeps within sight and sound of each other. But don't bunch up, especially on downhills, or there'll be some rear-end wipe-outs. And they can be real nasty! It's always a good idea to wait for stragglers at the top of climbs, at the bottom of tricky descents and at gates. It's in the nature of a strung out group to separate even further at such points so make sure that the young, eager pup out in front is aware of it.

One of the first signs of fatigue is when your normally ebullient companion rides quiet and persistently lags behind. Don't push it. Rest, drink, eat and keep warm – exposure may be just around the corner. Prevention is better than cure. Eat heartily a few hours before you set out and eat lots of carbohydrates. If you expect to be riding for more than a couple of hours then make full use of the various sports recovery drinks and carbo-loading preparations now available – after all you're just as deserving of their benefits as the athletes who advertise the stuff. Try not to ride for more than an hour without having some food – not as easy as it sounds – and drink regularly and drink plenty, before you get thirsty. Don't be over-confident when assessing how much trail should pass under your tyres during the day. Take into account the amount of height to be climbed – it's more important than mileage! The times given with each route are a guide and do not allow for stops. Even the terminally-fit will find that thirty-odd miles or about 4000ft of height-gain is about as much as they want to do in one day.

Weather

Out in the wilds, weather will make or break a ride. Outside of mid-summer you can be subjected to sun, sleet, rain, wind, warmth, cold and calm all in the space of a day out in the Dales. Maybe our highlands are minor mounds on the world map but it can be as bleak as Arctic tundra up on the Pennines when winter gets a grip. Howgill is derived from High-gill but might better be called Howl-gill when a storm's brewing! It's easy to be lulled into a false sense of security, set out ill-informed and unprepared and end up the subject of a fell rescue operation. Get the most recent weather forecast and make a habit of catching the latest TV weather forecasts. They give a useful overview of what's coming.

Three factors that strangers to the high moors often fail to take into account are altitude, wind and winter. As you climb, temperature falls. Roughly speaking, temperature falls one degree centigrade for every 100m gain in height (3C° per 1000ft) on a clear day, half that fall on a cloudy one. Wind-chill increases with wind strength. In a gentle to moderate breeze (Force 3, about 10mph) wind-chill is about -5C°, about -10C° in a fresh, gusty breeze

(Force 5, about 20mph) and -15C° in a really strong wind (Force 7, about 30mph).

It would be foolish to venture out onto the hilltops if gale-force winds are forecast knowing that they'll be more ferocious on the higher fells. Take a furlough and live to bike another day. And be prepared to take an unplanned detour if the weather deteriorates badly while you're out.

Losing your way

Navigation can be tricky. Keeping on course depends on you, and preferably your companions as well, knowing your position at ALL times. Danger zones are forests, open moor and poor visibility, so take care to read the terrain correctly in these situations and make no assumptions about this or that trail being a 'main' route. One way of coping with poor visibility is to follow a compass bearing to the most distant visible marker, cycle to it, take another bearing on the next marker, cycle and so on. Most of the routes described take you along obvious tracks so you are more likely to feel lost than really be lost.

But, despite our best endeavours to keep you on track, there's always a chance you might wander from the route. Nobody intends to get lost and it comes as a shock. Don't panic. Stop. Regroup. Make sure everybody's with you, then keep together and only then try to work out where you went wrong. Not too far back you'll have been sure of your position. Find it on the map.

Naturally you'll have been using your cycle computer to keep a log of point-to-point distances and it's a simple matter of reading off the distance and determining direction to get an approximate position. Forgotten to zero the trip distance at the last known point? Then estimate how long ago you were there and in which direction you have travelled during the elapsed time. Allowing for ground conditions, calculate how far you've cycled. Now check your surroundings and see if local landmarks coincide with your findings. If you're still unsure and visibility is poor then stay put until conditions improve.

In an ideal world three distinct landmarks should be recognised for you to be absolutely certain of your locality though, given two, you can still take compass bearings to position yourself. It goes without saying that correct use of the compass and trusting it, not your instincts, is vital. Many people get lost because they start navigating by guesswork instead of compass-work.

Fitness

Being fit is not just a question of muscle power. It's as much about recovery rate and in the Yorkshire Dales some of the climbs are big. Legs that are quick to revive are not just an asset but, on longer routes, a necessity. Being in shape to take a mountain bike off-road in a landscape as rugged as this is takes time to develop. That's because fitness gains are made during the periods of rest between spells of activity. No rest and no gain. This also means that you can't significantly increase your fitness levels in an uninterrupted session of trail-blazing. You need time. So if you're treating yourself to an off-road spree, slot in a couple of days furlough to allow that extra fitness to build.

Companions

A day riding rough stuff will be an enriched experience if you're in good company. A well-integrated team are much better able to overcome adversities with ease; even if it's a simple thing like bad weather. Not always so simple! But trail companions are notoriously tricky to choose and in the ups and downs betwixt the beginning and end of the day there will be stresses and strains. Off-roading is not all fun. On precipitous trails it's both difficult and demanding; add fatigue, perhaps a misread map and a ferocious wind and you've got a pretty good recipe for a falling out. Always distressing, discord can soon develop into dispute and that could be dangerous, in the wrong place at the wrong time. Choose companions carefully. It goes without saying that you should all get on but don't forget fitness. One mis-match – couch potato or fitness freak – in an otherwise well-balanced band of bikers will often lead to persistent friction and cast a shadow over the whole party.

Bike care

BEFORE RIDING: A routine check-up should include brake blocks, tyres, wheels and gears. It's a good idea to keep an eye on the chain, headset, stem, cranks and seat post. Don't forget to lube the chain.

AFTER RIDING: Treat your bike kindly and it'll be a reliable friend. At the end of a day hammering and being hammered on Dales trails the last thing you want to do is bike maintenance but at the very least you should clean (a quick wash with soapy water should suffice), lube (a dose of water-displacer followed by oil on the chain) then check it over. Do this right after a ride and you'll remember all those little mechanicals that have been niggling you during the ride plus wet mud washes off easily, dried mud is a lot harder to shift.

Trail-side fix fixers

BROKEN GEAR CABLES: You'll be left with a granny ring (front) or small sprocket (rear). Use the high/low adjusters to shift the mech to a middle gear.

TOTALLED REAR MECH: Split the chain and remove the mech entirely. Put the chain round the middle chainring and a middle sprocket. Rejoin it, discarding sufficient links to take up slack, and you'll have a single-speed clunker.

SPLIT TYRE: Usually caused by a rubbing brake block. Stop at once. Deflate and remove tyre bead from the rim on the damaged side. Place a bank note behind the split on the inside of the tyre with a margin folded over the bead of the tyre so it'll be wedged against the rim when the tube's re-inflated. Pump up and ride carefully.

TACCOED WHEEL: Remove the tyre then use brute force to push the offending bows back in line. Rest two apexes on opposite sides of the rim on two logs or rocks, the bow curving away from the contact point. Grab opposite sides of the rim and shove down. Only one log or rock handy? Then wedge a bowed out section of the wheel against it – or a tree – at an angle, rest the opposite sector on your knees or body and shove. Hard! No handy tree or boulder? Then whack the apex of a bow on the ground, refit the wheel, adjust with a spoke key, refit the tyre and ride very carefully. If you still have to disengage the brake in order to ride then it's probably better to leg it.

PUNCTURE – NO REPAIR KIT: Remove inner tube, cut/split across puncture and tie the resulting ends together. Partially inflate before replacing and refitting tyre.

Accident procedure

It's vital that at least one of the party is a qualified first aider. Ideally all of you should know the fundamentals of first aid. The British Red Cross, St John's Ambulance and St Andrew's Ambulance Societies all run courses.

It can't be over-emphasised that carrying a proper first aid kit with instructions and being a competent first aider is an essential part of accident procedure. But first aid instructions don't always cover the common illnesses and injuries associated with wild country mountain biking. These are given below:

HYPOTHERMIA / EXPOSURE (*The most common cause for rescue calls*)

Symptoms	Complaints of fatigue, cold, visual abnormalities
	Lethargy, lack of interest
	Cold, clammy skin, pale in colour
	Slurred speech
	Cramps
	Clumsiness
	Odd behaviour, out of character actions
	Collapse and coma
	Assume exposure if two or more of these symptoms are apparent and treat immediately
Action	Stop. Do not continue in the hope that you'll find shelter.
	Shelter the patient. Wrap them in extra clothing and put them in the survival bag, with someone else if possible. If you have a sleeping bag then use it as an inner layer.
	Warm the patient with bodily companionship and a warm drink if possible. Easily digested energy food can be given providing the patient is not too drowsy.
	Cheer the patient up – low morale is a contributory factor. Be positive – the rest of the group will be feeling pretty worried.
	Rest the patient for a prolonged period. If there's any doubt about the patient's ability to recover then send for help.
	Look for signs of exposure in other members of the party and signs of frostbite if conditions are severe.
	Do not rub the patient to restore circulation.

Do not give alcohol – it may cause collapse.

Extreme cases sometimes stop breathing so be pre–pared to give mouth to mouth and if the patient does lose consciousness place them in the recovery position.

FROSTBITE *(Big descents after a long stop or fierce winds in winter are likely causes)*

Symptoms
Prickling pain
Numbness
Skin may discolour blue or white
Skin may feel hard

Action
Warm the affected area with additional body heat only. Extremities are the most commonly affected areas and can be placed in the armpit or crotch. The face can be smothered with dry, gloved hands.

Remove rings, watches, boots etc. to ensure free blood flow.

Return to civilisation and get the patient to hospital if at all possible or get help.

Do not rub the affected area.

Do not apply heat from an artificial source.

Do not use re-vitalised limb or the affected tissue will tear. Again **SEEK MEDICAL HELP.**

HEAT EXHAUSTION *(Common during periods of sustained effort)*

Symptoms
Pale, sweaty skin
Cramps
Complaints of dizziness, fatigue and headache
Rapid but weak pulse, shallow breathing
Fainting

Action
Shade the patient. Find a cool, shady spot and lie them down.

Cold drinks of water, slightly salted and with a little sugar if available, will soon aid recovery.

SEEK MEDICAL HELP.

HEAT-STROKE *(Severe heat exhaustion)*

Symptoms
Restlessness
Frequent passing of urine
Complaints of dizziness and headache
Hot, flushed, dry skin
Rapid, strong pulse
Fainting

Action
Cool patient quickly by laying them in the shade and removing their clothes.

Sponge their body with a cloth soaked in water until

their body temperature drops and they appear to recover.
SEEK MEDICAL HELP IMMEDIATELY.

SHOCK *(Present in almost all cases of traumatic accidents)*

Symptoms

Pale and pallid skin, especially the lips
Rapid, weak pulse
Rapid, shallow breathing
Cold, sweaty skin
Complaints of dizziness and blurred vision
Restlessness
Yawning, pronounced sighing
Fainting

Action

Reassure the patient.
External bleeding or other injuries should be treated simultaneously.
Lay the patient down, protected from the ground and elements if it's cold, avoiding unnecessary movement.
TURN their head to one side.
Raise their feet on a pile of clothes or small rucksack.
Loosen restrictive clothing.
Control body temperature with loose clothing.
SEEK MEDICAL HELP IMMEDIATELY.
DO NOT GIVE FOOD OR DRINK.
DO NOT APPLY HEAT FROM AN ARTIFICIAL SOURCE.

DISLOCATION (Elbow, shoulder and knee joints are most at risk)

Symptoms

Deformity of the joint, especially when compared to the joint on the opposite side of the body
Swelling around the joint
Lack of mobility
Severe pain associated with the joint

Action

Support the injured limb in a comfortable position. Use the triangular bandage for arm/shoulder dislocations when the patient can sit or stand, rolled up clothes for the leg.
SEEK MEDICAL HELP.
DO NOT try to manipulate the joint.
DO NOT MOVE the affected joint unnecessarily.

BROKEN COLLAR BONE *(Perhaps the most common MTB fracture)*

Symptoms

Patient supports injured arm against the body
Head inclined towards the injured shoulder
Lack of mobility in the injured side
Swelling at the front of injured shoulder

Action Position arm of injured side with fingers up towards the opposite shoulder, palm flat against the body, so far as the patient will allow. Place soft padding between the upper arm and body.

Support the arm using the triangular bandage for an elevation sling off the good shoulder that encloses the elbow, forearm and hand.

Secure the arm against the body with a belt or rucksack strap that encircles the body.

SEEK MEDICAL HELP.

DO NOT MOVE the injured arm if it is too painful, support against the body in situ.

ROUTE DIRECTIONS, ABBREVIATIONS AND INSTRUCTIONS

Instructions are brief and to the point and follow a uniform format that is designed to give least hindrance on the trail.

The following abbreviations are used:

SO   straight on/over

L   left

R   right

LH   left-hand

RH   right-hand

Routes are split into small sections of usually less than 5.0m/8.7km that fall between natural stopping points such as gates and major junctions where it is convenient to zero the 'trip' distance on your cycle computer (re-setting your computer at regular intervals reduces the divergence between your computer display and the distances given in the directions below).

Primary compass bearings are given in brackets where directions need further clarification and distances are given in miles and kilometres.

A straightforward route instruction for one of these point-to-point sections is described in one sentence as shown below:

"Go SO to gate into Cow Gill farm at 3.75m/6km."

Despite the improved quality of signing and waymarking some off-road routes are not easy to follow so additional information is attached. This may include through-junctions, major direction changes, fords, technical obstacles etc. together with their distance from the last point where you will have zeroed your trip distance. This additional information is provided as a running check on your point-to-point progress:

"…(on bridleway track at first), forking L (S) at T-junction at 0.7m/1.15km (onto technical singletrack) and following cairns from 2.3m/3.7km."

Placed together the complete instruction gives you the direction to set off in, running information, your destination (where you will next zero the computer's 'trip' distance) and its distance from you:

"Go SO (on bridleway track at first), forking L at T-junction at 0.7m/1.15km (onto technical singletrack) and following cairns from 2.3m/3.7km to gate into Cow Gill farm at 3.75m/6km."

INSTRUCTIONS

SCALE

The maps used are based upon the Ordnance Survey 1:50 000 Landranger series which have been reduced by approximately 20 per cent. Each grid square represents 0.6miles/1km square.

The Landranger from which each map is taken is indicated at the start of each route.

SWALEDALE

A winter's trail — snow-bound track in Upper Swaledale

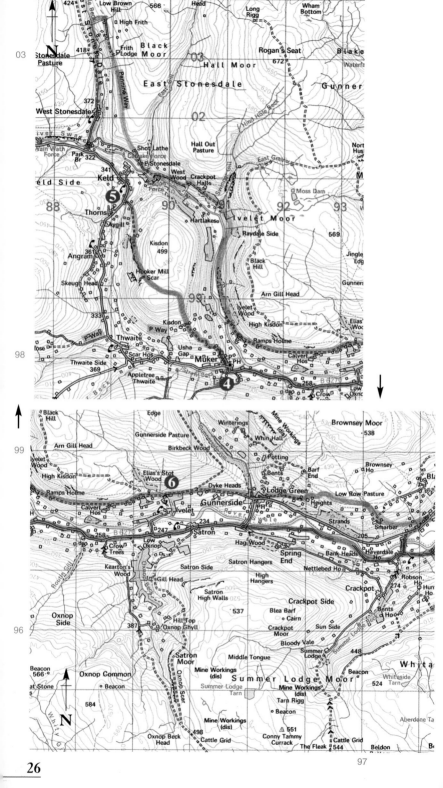

EXPERT Route 1
SWALEDALE

A brilliant summer's day ride with plenty of scope to tailor it to suit shorter times. It's quite a climb up to Apedale Head but the 1000ft (300m) drop back down to the Swale is an entertaining mix-and-match batch of singletrack, road and rutted track. It's easy to over-shoot the field gate accessing the track down to Low Houses. From there to Kisdon it's pootle-time with an opportunity to down a pint in Muker. Kisdon marks a return to granny-cogging; height-gain is impressive as are the views down Swaledale. Suddenly it all turns Pennine-like on top – bleak, far-flung fells surround – before the trail bounces down to Keld.

A tarmac interlude sets you up for a scenic saunter down the Pennine Way. If it's a fine summer's afternoon you're in for some real soul biking from here on in. The track past Crackpot is one of the best bits of biking along The Coast-to-Coast cycle route; once a simple cart track it makes for an exciting roller-coaster ride with tricky climbs and enough rough stuff to make top-cogging on

DISTANCE
35 miles (56km)
HEIGHT-GAIN
3930ft (1200m)
TIME
6hrs (dry)
7.5hrs (wet)
NAVIGATION
SKILLS
moderate
RIDE DIRECTION
clockwise

A roller-coaster route over the heights of Kisdon and Whitaside with some prime-time gnarly bits for kicks. Features part of The Coast-to-Coast off-road cycle route.

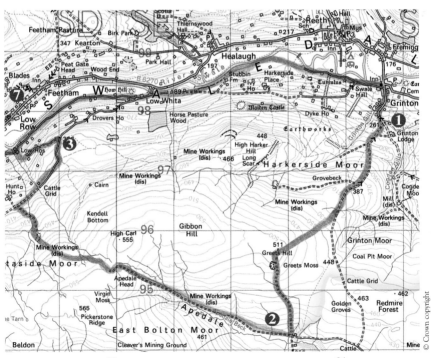

descents a touch risky. Watch out for the gate down by Swinner Gill though! The valley's verdant, the views gorgeous – literally! And if you're tempted to forgo the climb up past Heights then think again; especially on a summer's evening. There's no better spot from which to see Swaledale.

❶ Start at Grinton YHA (GR048976) and from entrance zigzag R/L (effectively SO, W) onto bridleway, turning L onto C-road at 0.12m/0.2km, forking R (SW) onto waymarked bridleway on How Hill at 1.1m/1.75km (singletrack faint at first), passing twin cairns on Greets Hill then swinging L after gate at 1.9m/3km to track T-junction at Dent's Houses at 2.8m/4.5km.

❷ Turn R on Apedale Head track, turning L at 2.2m/3.5km and swinging R past large cairn to go through gate in fence at 2.3m/3.7km. Swing R, soon to swing L (W) through tips on boggy singletrack then swinging R (NW) onto track at 0.9m/1.5km, turning R at T-junction with C-road at 1.4m/2.25km (over cattle grid) to gate at High Lane at 2.25m/3.6km.

❸ Turn L through gate, across field then through RH gate onto track to T-junction with C-road in Low Houses at 0.5m/ 0.8km. Turn L, keeping SO at T-junction at 0.3m/0.5km, forking R at 'dead-end' T-junction at Haverdale at 0.5m/0.8km onto Dubbing Garth Lane to B6270 at 2.4m/3.8km. Keep SO to Muker then turning R at 2.5m/4km into Muker and zigzagging L/R onto waymarked bridleway track to gate at Ford at 2.7m/4.3km.

❹ Go through (N then W), track zigzags at first then forking R at

0.5m/0.8km up walled track, keeping SO at 0.7m/1.15km by wall on L to gate at 0.8m/1.3km. Go SO, keeping to wall on R to corner then turning L on gated grass singletrack, joining gated track at 0.5m/0.8km near sheepfold and crossing ford at 1.4m/2.2km to B6270 at 1.5m/2.4km.

❺ Turn R, past Keld, turning R over bridge at T-junction at 0.75m/1.2km, turning R at T-junction with bridleway track at 1.6m/2.6km and soon keeping L on to bridleway to T-junction with Pennine Way at 2.25m/3.6km. Turn R through gate, forking R at T-junction at 0.3m/0.5km to East Stonesdale farm at 1.5m/2.4km. Go SO (crossing gated farmyard), passing T-junction where Pennine Way turns R at 0.1m/0.15km, keeping R at Crackpot fork at 0.75m/1.2km, joining road at Ramps Holme farm at 2.7m/4.3km to T-junction near Ivelet at 4m/6.4km.

❻ Turn L, keeping SO on B6270 X-roads in Gunnerside at 1.1m/1.75km to steel gate on L at 1.25m/2km. Fork L up drive (keeping L of house then on to walled singletrack bridleway), leaving Heights Ho to R at 0.4m/0.6km (then singletrack keeps topside of wall), swinging L (N) at 0.5m/0.8km up field before swinging R through gate at 0.6m/1km. Keep SO to 1st wall corner at

0.5m/0.8km, turning R (between walls) to Smarber, keeping L, through gate then following track (E) to T-junction with B6270 in Low Row at 0.75m/1.2km.

❼ Turn R, turning L at first T-junction at 0.25m/0.4km, across bridge, L at next T-junction at 0.6m/1km to Low Houses at 0.9m/1.4km. Fork L on Low Lane track, joining C-road at 1.5m/2.4km and keeping SO at T-junction at 1.7m/2.7km (over cattle grid) to T-junction with singletrack bridleway off L at 2.2m/3.5km. Turn L (NNE) for 50yds/45m to go through gate. Swing R on gated singletrack below Stubbins Farm, joining C-road by Swale Hall at 1.8m/2.9km, turning R in Grinton at 2.1m/3.4km and keeping SO at T-junction at 2.5m/4km to Grinton YHA and start at 2.7m/4.3km.

SPORT Route 2 REETH MOOR
FUN Route 3 LOW ROW

DISTANCE
25 miles (40km)
HEIGHT-GAIN
3500ft (1060m)
TIME
4hrs (dry)
5hrs (wet)
NAVIGATION
SKILLS
moderate
RIDE DIRECTION
either way

Scoot round the old mining tracks of Marrick and Reeth, a jaunt across Melbecks Moor finishing off with a heady mix of techno-track and scenic sauntering down the dale home.

DISTANCE
15 miles (24km)
HEIGHT-GAIN
950ft (290m)
TIME
1.5hrs (dry)
2.5hrs (wet)
NAVIGATION
SKILLS:
easy
RIDE DIRECTION
either way

An ideal low-level route for beginners but take care on the tarmac sections, especially in summer. In the wet be prepared for mud and enormous puddles.

Thankfully there's tarmac up to Fremington Edge; its 1000ft (300m) vantage gives fine views over the dales down below. A thriving mining industry has left a legacy of mining tracks for us to ride and it is one of these that we join at the road end. Puddled and pot-holed it's fun to ride, especially the twisty dip down into Storthwaite Farm. But be sure to follow route directions carefully – tracks are numerous and it's easy to be misled in the mist. On Great Pinseat there isn't a single blade of grass; it's an eerie setting, especially when mists swirl and curl around – acres of dead white spoil heaps where lead has left the soil bereft of life. Makes ideal riding though!

More meandering mine tracks – with the occasional dip and dive to liven things up – take you round to Blakenthwaite's craggy cleft in the heather. It's a steep drop down, round the valley head to the gill. Then things turn a touch technical, singletrack rules for a time then it's back to track – this time with gravity on your side – all the way down to Gunnerside; nearly! You'll have to weigh up the pros and cons of the optional hoick over the Heights – I like it for the views.

❶ Start in Reeth (GR038993). Take B6270 (E, towards Grinton), forking L at T-junction on RH bend in Low Fremington at 0.6m/1km, almost immediately forking L on lane, turning L at 0.75m/1.2km into High Fremington and zigzagging L/R at 0.8m/1.3km up to gate at 1.25m/2km. Go SO over Fremington Edge to Hurst Farm at 1.5m/2.4km.

❷ Turn L on bridleway track, swinging L (W) onto singletrack at 0.8m/1.3km, swinging R by fence to gate on inside of corner at 1m/1.6km. Go SO through gate (following singletrack through tips), swinging L then R at 0.5m/0.8km to gate at 1m/1.6km. Go SO, turning R by Storthwaite Hall Farm at

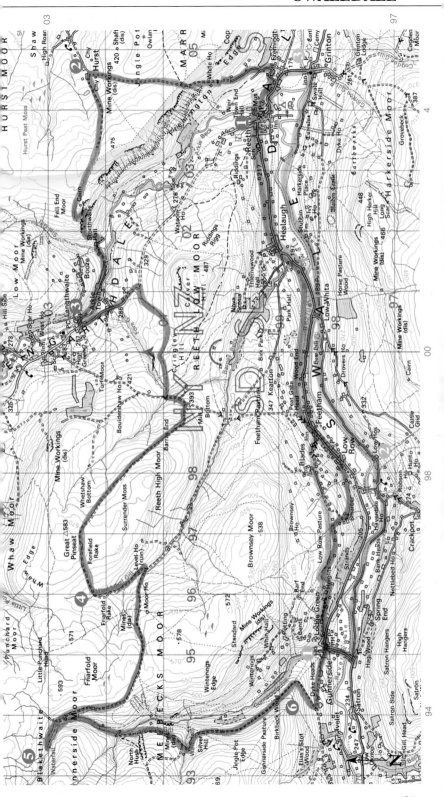

0.15m/0.25km on track to Langthwaite at 1m/1.6km.

❸ Turn L (immediately over bridge), turning L (towards Raw) to waymarked T-junction with bridleway at 0.75m/1.2km. Turn R, swinging R then L round spur to T-junction with C-road at Fore Gill gate at 1.4m/2.2km. Turn L through ford, turning R onto bridleway track at T-junction at 0.4m/0.6km, swinging L (NW) by sheepfold at 2m/3.2km over Great Pinseat tips and following cairns from 2.25m/3.6km then descending L (W) to go through gate at 2.7m/4.3km.

❹ Turn L (through ford then down track), turning R (over Level Ho Bridge) at 0.6m/1km, through tips on bridleway track and keeping SO (W) at T-junction at 1m/1.6km, keeping R at T-junction at 1.75m/2.8km and turning L (NW then W) at T-junction with singletrack (vague, head up valley) by fords at Blakenthwaite Mines at 3m/4.8km to dam at 3.2m/5.1km.

❺ Take hairpin turn L (Care! Steep drop to stream before joining technical singletrack), forking R at T-junction at 0.75m/1.2km, over ford and picking up track at North Hush to T-junction with C-road at Dyke Heads at 3.6m/5.8km.

❻ Turn L, keeping SO on B6270 at X-roads in Gunnerside at 1.1m/1.75km to steel gate on L at 1.25m/2km. Fork L up drive (keeping L of house then on to walled singletrack bridleway), leaving Heights Ho to R at 0.4m/0.6km (then singletrack keeps topside of wall), swinging L (N) at 0.5m/0.8km up field before swing-

ing R through gate at 0.6m/1km. Keep SO to 1st wall corner at 0.5m/0.8km, turning R (between walls) to Smarber, keeping L, through gate then following track (E) to T-junction with B6270 in Low Row at 0.75m/1.2km. Fork L back to start in Reeth at 4m/6.4km.

❶ Start Gunnerside (GR951982). Take B6270 (towards Muker and Keld), crossing bridge, turning L at T-junction at 0.4m/0.6km, almost immediately forking L into Dubbing Garth Lane track, joining C-road at 2.1m/3.4km and going SO at T-junction at 2.25m/3.6km to lane end at Low Houses at 2.6m/4.1km.

❷ Fork L (on Low Lane track), joining C-road at 1.5m/2.4km, keeping SO at T-junction at 1.7m/2.7km and over cattle grid to T-junction with singletrack bridleway off L at 2.2m/3.5km. Turn L for 50yds/45m to go through gate. Swing R on gated singletrack below Stubbins Farm, joining C-road by Swale Hall at 1.8m/2.9km to T-junction in Grinton at 2.1m/3.4km.

❸ Turn L, going SO onto B6270 at 50yds/45m and passing through Reeth and Healaugh to T-junction with C-road in Feetham just past Punchbowl Inn at 4.5m/7.2km. Fork R, joining bridleway track at 0.8m/1.3km and going SO at track junction at 1m/1.6km to go through gate at 1.5m/2.4km. Zigzag L/R downhill, passing Heights Ho, joining walled track then singletrack and keeping L on lane at 0.6m/1km and through gate to B6270 in Gunnerside at 0.8m/1.3km. Fork R back to start at 0.12m/0.2km.

WENSLEYDALE

Climbing the Roman Road out of Bainbridge, Wensleydale (Route 6)

FUN Route 4
BOLTON MOOR

DISTANCE
16 miles (26km)
HEIGHT-GAIN
1880ft (570m)
TIME
2.5hrs (dry)
3hrs (wet)
NAVIGATION
SKILLS
moderate
RIDE DIRECTION
clockwise

*A double dose of
scenics in this dale-
to-dale hop that
finales with a couple
of prime-time track
runs*

Farm track that contours for the most part gives your limbs time to warm up before a touch of tarmac torture – the climb over The Fleak. Don't ignore the views opening out behind – they're an ideal excuse to stop and give the heart-rate time to simmer down. The drop off The Fleak is fast and furious. Twisty too; take care!

After all that freewheeling slipstream roar on the steep sweep into Swaledale the tricky track climb up to Apedale Head comes as a bit of a shock. But once you're up – watch the wheel-grabbers along the singletrack on top – it's downhill all the way home; nearly! Apedale has a couple of unexpected ups to give the legs a work-out. Do a right at Dents, crest Black Hill and relax for some prime-time track cruising back to Bolton.

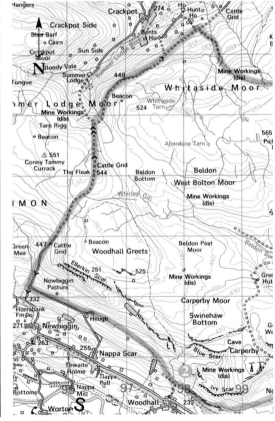

96   99

❶ Start Castle Bolton car park (GR033919). Turn R (W on gated track), swinging L through gate onto bridleway grass track at 1.6m/2.6km, forking L (towards Askrigg) at signed bridleway T-junction at 2.1m/3.4km, going SO fields and joining track at 3.6m/5.75km to go through gate at 4.1m/6.6km.

❷ Zigzag L/R (Effectively SO and immediately joining track, later walled) then keeping R at T-junction at 1.4m/2.2km to T-junction with C-road at 2m/3.2km. Turn R (steep and twisty descent into Swaledale – take care!), turning R (S, towards Castle Bolton) at T-junction with bridleway track at 3.4m/5.5km, keeping SO (SSE) at T-junction at 4.1m/6.6km (following cairns now), swinging R at 4.8m/7.7km to go through gate at Apedale Head at 5.0m/8km.

❸ Go SO, immediately swinging L at large cairn (on muddy track) and swinging R again, turning right at track X-roads at Dent's Houses at 2.3m/3.7km and joining walled track at 3.7m/5.9km to T-junction with C-road in Castle Bolton at 3.8m/6.1km. Turn R back to start at 0.1m/0.15km.

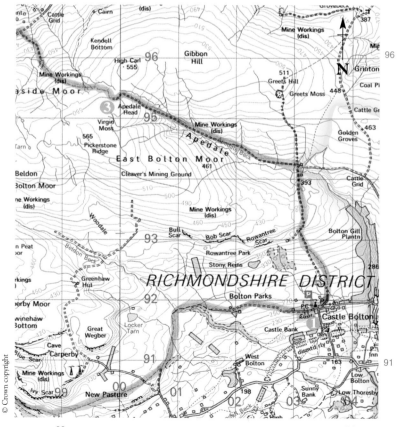

SPORT Route 5
DODD FELL

DISTANCE
13 miles (21km)
HEIGHT-GAIN
1350ft (410m)
TIME
2hrs (dry)
2.5hrs (wet)
NAVIGATION
SKILLS
easy/moderate
RIDE DIRECTION
either way

Short and sweet, the meat of this loop lies in the contour-hopping climb (or descent) above Burtersett. An ideal mate for an Expert figure of eight with Route 7.

Basically a one up and one down this loop begs to be ridden both ways. As written the road ride allows a warm-up before the lung-busting climb from Burtersett. It's technical too – ruts and rubble conspire to give grip the slip and getting started again is a trial of power control. As a downhill, wheel-grabbing ruts are set to test both nerve and skill. Don't wander onto Wether Fell – the obvious path heads straight across then peters out amidst peat hag. The bridleway keeps by the inside of the northern wall but even that has its hazards; abrupt drop-offs and a few dips that call for a 100 per cent commit-and-crank routine. On an anti-clockwise loop, watch out for stone steps about 1m/1.6km from Cam High Road. Half the loop follows the Pennine Way so please ride with consideration towards walkers.

❶ Start Gayle Beck Bridge, Gayle (GR871893). Take C-road (ENE, towards A684 and Bainbridge), soon turning R on A684 (busy road!), turning R (towards Burtersett) at T-junction with minor road at 1.2m/1.9km, forking R at T-junction at 1.4m/2.3km in Burtersett and turning L at T-junction with bridleway track at 1.5m/2.4km to gate at 1.6m/2.5km.

❷ Go through gate (obvious track zigzags R then L, gets steep and very rough), cresting col at 1m/1.6km, turning R at T-junction (with footpath) at 1.12m/1.8km, keeping R at T-junction with vague bridleway at 1.25m/2km and keeping L at T-junction with singletrack at 1.4m/2.2km to go through gate onto Wether Fell at 1.4m/2.3km. Fork R (keeping alongside wall on vague singletrack at first) and turning R at signed bridleway/track T-junction at 1.4m/2.2km to T-junction with C-road at 2.3m/3.7km.

❸ Fork L, keeping R at T-junction at 0.4m/0.6km (onto gated road) to T-junction with Pennine Way (signpost) bridleway track just after Kidhow Gate at 2.7m/4.3km. Turn R, forking R at singletrack T-junction (Pennine Way waymarker) at 2.3m/3.75km

to go through gate on to Gaudy House drive at 4.1m/6.6km. Turn R (drainage runnels!), turning L at next T-junction, keeping R at T-junction at 0.4m/0.6km, turning R (towards Gayle) at T-junction at 0.5m/0.8km and keeping SO at junctions that follow to start at 0.8m/1.3km.

© Crown copyright

SPORT Route 6
GREEN SCAR

FUN Route 7
SEMER WATER

DISTANCE
14.5 miles (23km)
HEIGHT-GAIN
1650ft (500m)
TIME
2.5hrs (dry), 3hrs (wet)
NAVIGATION
SKILLS
easy
RIDE DIRECTION
either way

A real Dales trail taster. A lot of track, a touch of technical and prospects set to make the mind wonder. Add it to Route 5 for an Expert 'eight'.

DISTANCE
12 miles (19km)
HEIGHT-GAIN
1300ft (400m)
TIME
2.5hrs (dry), 3hrs (wet)
NAVIGATION
SKILLS
easy
RIDE DIRECTION
either way

A version of Route 6 with the technical taken out. Take care on the tarmac descents – all sport some seriously sharp bends!

Climbing the old Roman Road out of Bainbridge is a case of mind over matter – a helmet peak helps. It doesn't test the legs until the very last so just keep plugging along. Once on top things liven up and the views over Semer Water strive for your attention as you tackle the techno-singletrack descent down to Countersett. The rough stuff's not nearly so dangerous as the switchbacks on the road though!

From Semer there's a long, measured climb back up to Stake Allotments. Mostly track this makes for an exciting, non-technical, top-cog descent if you're riding the loop clockwise. Half-way down to Carpley Green Farm the track hangs a left, steepens and gets rough. Ideal pinch-puncture territory if you're hammering! Again, watch out on the twisty tarmac at the end.

❶❶ Start top side of Bainbridge green (GR934902). Leave village on minor C-road (S, towards Countersett and Semer Water), keeping R (on to track) at T-junction at 0.75m/1.2km to track/C-road X-roads at 2.2m/3.5km.

❷ Turn L on C-road (over hill) to gate on sharp LH bend on descent at 0.75m/ 1.2km to pick up Sport Route at para No 3.

❷ Go SO, turning L at gated T-junction with bridleway at 1.5m/2.4km (on grass track), soon swinging L through gate, going SO at finger-posted T-junc-

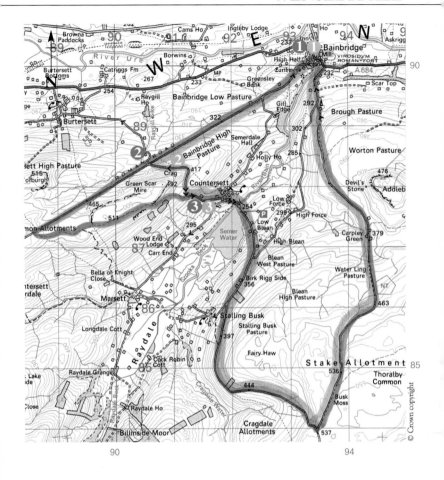

tion at 2.1m/3.4km, keeping L at vague singletrack T-junction at 2.25m/3.6km (soon after gate) then climbing over to gate at 2.9m/4.6km. Go through gate and swing R (down twisty, rough singletrack) and through gate at 0.5m/0.8km to C-road at 0.6m/1km.

❸❸ Turn R, zigzagging R/L (effectively SO) at staggered X-roads in Countersett at 0.5m/0.8km

(sharp RH bend after bridge!), keeping R (towards Stalling Busk) at T-junction at 1.1m/1.75km and forking L onto High Lane track at 1.6m/2.6km to track T-junction with signpost on Busk Moss at 3.75m/6km. Turn L (on green lane), joining tarmac after Carpley Green farm (sharp bends!), keeping R at T-junction at 3.8m/6.1km and turning L on A684 at 4.15m/6.6km back into Bainbridge and the start at 4.6m/7.4km.

LANGSTROTHDALE

Dropping down to Yockenthwaite, Langstrothdale (Route 10)

EXPERT Route 8
LANGSTROTHDALE AND OUGHTERSHAW

DISTANCE
38 miles (61km)
HEIGHT-GAIN
3680ft (1115m)
TIME
7hrs (dry)
9hrs (wet)
NAVIGATION SKILLS
easy
RIDE DIRECTION
clockwise

Almost a tour in its own right this ride meanders through the most remote regions in the Dales. Mostly track, the loop saves the best 'til last on the long drop to Buckden.

Longest route in the book but there's plenty of opt-outs so it's a loop without the pressure to complete. There's a long, tarmac intro into Green Field Forest then track that sweeps you almost effortlessly up 600ft (180m) onto Birkwith Moor. An entertaining, roller-coaster run down to Horton in Ribblesdale in the company of the Pennine Way (watch out for walkers) then a little-used lane climbs steadily up to Old Ing. 200yds (180m) N – just over the wall on the right – there's a pretty spectacular sink worth looking at.

The next mile or so – to Ling Gill Bridge (a beautiful spot that's been scheduled as a SSSI) – is rump-rattle track then the 4x4 boys get to grips with the trail and it's erosion run-riot, big time! Mega-ruts and puddles all the way up to the road out of Cam Houses. Sadly this was paved Roman road just a few years ago.

For a while the route shares tyre tracks with Sport Route 7, spins along the top of Stake Moss then amble-time abruptly ends in the shattered track that drops down to the Buckden road. Go too slow and you'll endo! A short, tarmac switchback then it's back to track across the fields where the ford below Cow Close is likely to unseat the unskilled. The fun finale is a skip 'n skid, top-cog descent down to Buckden but – and it's a big but – don't click in the big ring unless it's mid-week or late in the day. The climb up from the car park is Joe Public's ideal half-hour out with the dog. And a warning if it's wet; the pedestrian polished limestone is slicker than a snail trail.

❶ Start main entrance to Buckden car park (GR774943). Turn L on B6160, turning R at T-junction with track at 100yds/100m, turning R on C-road soon after, keeping L at T-junction at Hubberholme at 1.25m/2km and turning L at T-junction at 5m/8km to go through gate onto track at High Green Field at 8m/12.8km. Keep SO, forking L at T-

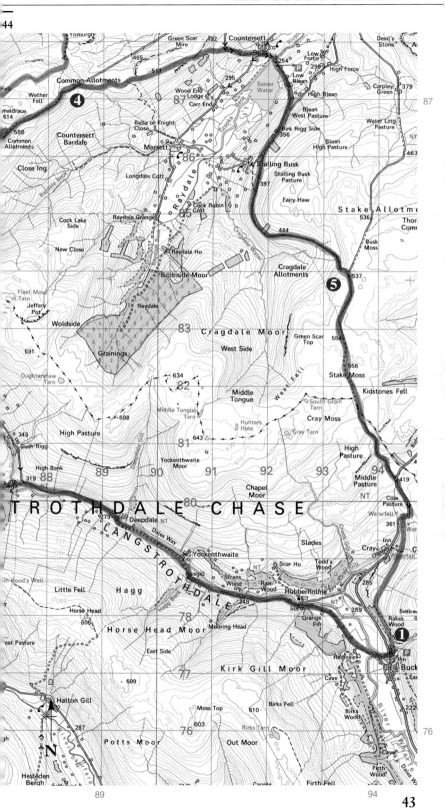

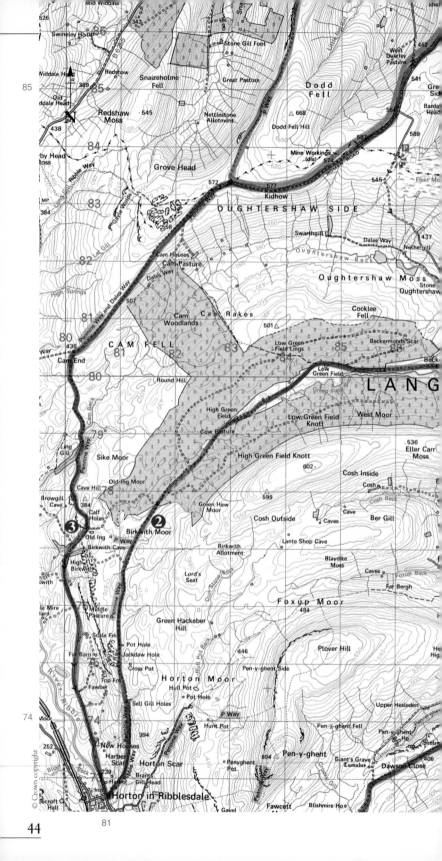

LANGSTROTHDALE

junction at 0.7m/1.15km to track T-junction with two gates at 1.25m/2km.

❷ Fork L through LH gate (Note: when Pennine Bridleway is instated and signed you can short-cut through RH gate for 1m/1.6km on track to T-junction at Old Ing), going SO (on bridleway), joining Pennine Way at T-junction at 0.4m/0.6km and keeping L at track T-junction with Ribble Way at 2.5m/8km to staggered X-roads with B6479 and C-road at 3.5m/8km. Turn R, on to C-road to High Birkwith and forking R at 2.75m/4.4km on track to T-junction with signpost at Old Ing at 3.2m/5.1km.

❸ Turn L (on gated track), crossing Ling Gill Bridge at 1m/1.6km, turning R at Cam End T-junction with signpost at 2.1m/3.4km (4x4 erosion gets worse from here on) and keeping L at T-junction with C-road at 4m/6.4km to Cold Keld Gate at 4.4m/7.1km. Go SO on gated unclassified road, keeping L at T-junction at 2.4m/3.8km and forking R through gate on to Cam High Road unclassified track at 2.9m/4.6km to gated bridleway T-junction (easy to overshoot; it's 0.2m/0.3km beyond sharp RH bend) at 4.8m/7.7km.

❹ Turn R (on grass track), soon swinging L through gate, going SO at finger-posted T-junction at 0.6m/1km, keeping L at vague singletrack T-junction at 0.75m/1.2km (soon after gate) then climbing over to gate at 1.4m/2.2km. Go through gate and swing R (down twisty, rough singletrack) and through gate at 0.5m/0.8km to C-road at 0.6m/1km. Turn R, zigzagging R/L at staggered X-roads in Countersett at 0.5m/0.8km (sharp RH bend after bridge!), keeping R (towards Stalling Busk) at T-junction at 1.1m/1.75km and forking L onto High Lane track at 1.6m/2.6km to track T-junction with signpost on Busk Moss at 3.75m/6km.

❺ Keep R (very rocky after 1.9m/3km), turning R down B6160 at 2.5m/4km, turning L at gated T-junction with bridleway (just after sharp RH bend) at 3m/4.8km and going through gate at 4.1m/6.6km (walkers – watch your speed!) down to start at 5.0m/8km.

SPORT Route 9
PEN-Y-GHENT

DISTANCE
18 miles (29km)
HEIGHT-GAIN
1750ft (530m)
TIME
3.5hrs (dry)
5hrs (wet)
NAVIGATION
SKILLS
easy/moderate
RIDE DIRECTION
either way

A big, big climb out of Littondale with a pernickety patch of loose stuff to circumnavigate at the outset then it's unremitting granny ring to the top. Triple tough in the wet! That's it! Big climb of the day bagged and the best is yet to come. Downhilling begins in earnest soon after rounding Churn Milk Hole. The track looks fit for a blast but this is where riders come to grief with alarming regularity. If the ruts don't get you the loose stuff surely will! And the lower you go the looser it gets! After that up pops a road and what do you do with all that surplus speed? From Helwith Bridge the road through Horton (cafe here) is busy with juggernauts but you escape soon enough on a gritty climb up to Hull Pot and that's where semi-technical, fun-time singletracking begins. Much is unride-

A loop around one of the Dales most famous peaks with a chance to see some huge holes, like Hull Pot; this Sport ride has hidden depths that have caught out even experienced riders. Foxup Moor suffers from wet-soil erosion; please use an alternative loop if the ground's gloopy and please note that there's a mile or so of permissive track on Foxup Moor; it is not a Right of Way.

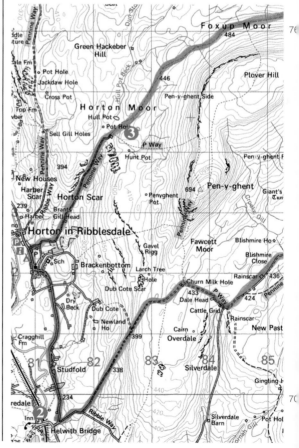

able in the wet so take heed of the caution already given in the introductory section of this book. There's a couple of tricky dips and one, as you begin the descent down to Foxup, is endo-inducing.

❶ Start New Bridge (GR897742). Cross River Skirfare on New Bridge, turning R up gated track and turning L at T-junction with C-road at Dawson Close at 3m/4.75km to T-junction with unclassified county road/Pennine Way by Dale Head farm at 4.25m/6.8km. Turn R (on Pennine Way at first), turning L by Churn Milk Hole at T-junction at 0.6m/1km to T-

3.5m/5.6km (on singletrack) and turning R (E) at 3.6m/5.8km to cross stile (just before Hull Pot; easy to fall into in poor visibility!) at 3.7m/5.9km.

❸ Swing L (NE), zigzagging L/R (effectively SO, alongside wall) at 0.3m/0.5km, zigzagging L/R (effectively SO, by signpost) at 2.5m/4km onto track to gate at 2.6m/4.2km. Go SO

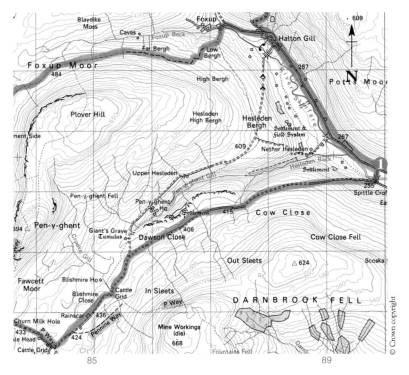

junction with B6480 at 2.6m/4.2km (watch your speed: wheel-grabbing ruts plus you'll shoot onto main road!).

❷ Turn R, turning R at T-junction with track in Horton-in-Ribblesdale at 2m/3.2km (up Pennine Way bridleway 75yds/70m before Tourist Information Centre/cafe), going SO through gate at track/singletrack X-roads at

(on permissive track with marker posts), forking L at 0.6m/1km, swinging L at 0.8m/1.3km, swinging L after going through gate at 0.9m/1.4km, joining bridleway and swinging L at 1.1m/1.75km (just after gate) to Foxup Farm at 1.3m/2.1km. Turn R on C-road, keeping L at T-junction at 0.75m/1.2km, turning R at T-junction with track to New Bridge at 2.3m/3.75km and turning R to start.

SPORT Route 10
HORSE HEAD MOOR

DISTANCE
12 miles (19km)
HEIGHT-GAIN
2200ft (660m).
TIME
2.5hrs (dry)
4hrs (wet)
NAVIGATION
SKILLS
easy
RIDE DIRECTION
clockwise

Technically extreme this double up and down route is destined to test trail skills to the limit and send you home with mud in your eye and adrenaline coursing through your veins.

The road ride to Halton Gill, where the off-road kicks in with a killer climb, is almost too short. On the ascent take time to pick your line round the first RH bend then hit turbo-boost; if you clear that then you've a good chance of making a clean climb. Then it's a wild ride down to Yockenthwaite. Finessing your way through the furrows is the best way to go, and watch out for grass-covered trenches on the singletrack run-out to the road.

Another gruelling climb – tougher than the last, especially if it's wet – takes you out of Wharfedale. Off the top the trail turns technical with steps, drop-offs and just plain old rough stuff to stretch your expertise. But be warned – there are hidden drop-offs so curb the speed and the cobbly bit near the bottom is an ice-rink in the wet.

❶ Start New Bridge (GR897742). At T-junction with C-road turn L, through Halton Gill, forking R at gated T-junction (signed Hawes) with unclassified track at 2m/3.2km going SO at Horse Head gate onto bridleway at 3.25m/5.25km (tricky descent starts soon) and swinging R at 4.5m/7.25km to C-road in Langstrothdale at 4.6m/7.4km.

❷ Turn R, keeping R at T-junction just before bridge at 1.25m/2km to T-junction with bridleway track at 2.2m/3.5km. Turn R, turning R at signed T-junction at 0.7m/1.15km and almost immediately going SO track X-roads (onto singletrack with marker posts) and swinging L (SSW) through gap in wall at 1.8m/2.9km

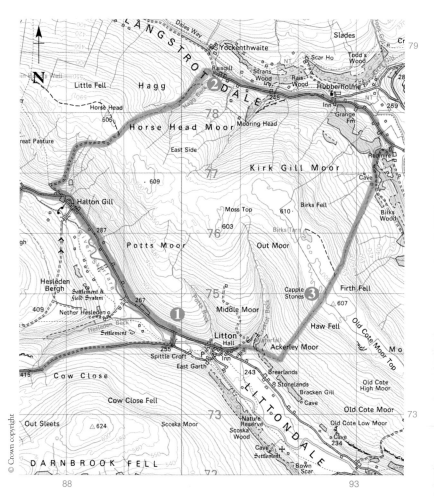

to go through gate on Firth Fell summit at 2.1m/3.4km.

❸ Go SO (SW, keeping near wall then drop-offs start at 0.2m/0.3km), zigzagging L/R (around dangerous 'edge') at 0.8m/1.3km and down gated track to go through field gate at 1.25m/2km. Swing L, turning R at T-junction with C-road in Litton at 0.3m/0.5km and turning L at T-junction at 1m/1.6km on track to New Bridge and the start.

MALHAM MOORS

Making mucky by Mastliles Gate, Malham (Route 11)

EXPERT Route 11
FOUNTAINS FELL

DISTANCE
33 miles (53km)
HEIGHT-GAIN
3300ft (1000m)
TIME
5hrs (dry)
7hrs (wet)
NAVIGATION
SKILLS
moderate/
difficult
RIDE DIRECTION
anticlockwise

Grand tour through gorgeous terrain that finishes with a 1000ft downhill fling for a finale.

The first off-road leg to Kilnsey is along the infamous Mastiles Lane. It was surfaced all the way once but recent adoption by powered vehicles has churned the top-most section to quagmire. Keep to the centre trenches even though they look the least inviting; top-stones pepper the margins where they lurk in the turf ready to topple the unwary rider. Some folk really rate the descent off Kilnsey Moor; it may be fast but that's about it. We take a short detour to take in a descent with more character – Green Haw Hill.

From Kilnsey it's a tarmac excursion up Littondale – reckoned by many to be the Dales most picturesque valley – to New Bridge. The starting point for Sport Route 10 which we follow almost all the way to Helwith Bridge. Just where the pell-mell track levels for a spell we take a left onto Moor Head Lane. It's a testing climb in the wet but pick the right rut and you'll make it to the top for a roller-coaster road ride to Streets cross-roads. This is where navigation skills are tested – sometimes the singletrack's a little vague but follow the directions and you should stay on track to Gorbeck's boggy byway. We zigzag to the top of Grizedales for some gratuitous downhilling all the way home. Watch for the slip in the wet and things get a touch rocky on the chicanes to the lane.

❶ Start Malham Bridge (GR901629). Head uphill past YHA (towards Malham Tarn) then forking R on track at 2m/3.2km to Street Gate at 2.2m/3.5km. Turn R through gate (alongside wall on your R) on Mastiles Lane unclassified county road, turning R at T-junction with bridleway at 2.2m/3.5km (just after gate), going SO bridleway/road X-roads at 2.8m/4.5km to X-roads with gated bridleways at 3.7m/5.9km. Turn L (NE), through R/L zigzag (effectively SO and heading N following marker posts), going through gate at 0.5m/0.8km, keeping L at T-junction at 0.75m/1.2km and keeping R at vague T-junction at 1.25m/2km to T-junction with Mastiles track at Howgill at 1.5m/2.4km.

❷ Turn R, keeping R at T-junctions at 0.25m/0.4km and 0.6m/1km to T-junction with B6160 in Kilnsey at 1m/1.6km. Turn L, over Skirfare Bridge, turning L at T-junction at 1m/1.6km (cattle grid) up Littondale (tea room in Hawkswick), through Litton and turning L at T-junction with unclassified county track at 6.9m/11km to gated T-junction (after crossing River Skirfare) at 7m/11.25km.

❸ Turn R up gated track and turning L at T-junction with C-road at Dawson Close at 3m/4.75km to T-junction with unclassified county road/Pennine Way by Dale Head farm at 4.25m/6.8km. Turn R (on Pennine Way at first), turning L by Churn Milk Hole at T-junction at 0.6m/1km to obvious track T-junction at 2.5m/4km (watch your speed or you'll overshoot!)

❹ Turn L on Moor Head Lane bridleway/unclassified county track, turning L on C-road at 1.4m/2.2km, turning R at T-junction (towards Malham) at 1.5m/2.4km, by Sannat Hall, going SO at next two T-junc-

tions and over cattle grid to Streets X-roads at 4.7m/7.5km.

❺ Take hairpin turn R (on very faint bridleway across field), going through gate at 0.1m/0.15km, swinging L (SW on bridleway singletrack; don't wander off on sheep trails), over stream, past marker-post and up singletrack to bridleway gate at 0.5m/0.8km. Go SO (W, beside broken wall at first), swinging L just before field corner, crossing another broken wall, over Black Hill col (on singletrack that does a lazy R/L swing for final 220yds/200m) to gate at 0.3m/0.5km. Go SO (WSW on bridleway singletrack) and turning L at T-junction with grass track at 0.4m/0.6km (110yds/100m E of a gate) to two gates at 1.3m/2.1km.

❻ Go through RH gate (down track), turning R (SW, just before gate) at 0.4m/0.6km, climbing over Grizedales (through three gates then up to and alongside wall) to T-junction with track by gate at 1.12m/1.8km. Turn L (down zigzag track), turning R on C-road at 1.25m/2km, going SO through gate on LH bend at 1.5m/2.4km (on faint bridleway across field at first then on walled lane), turning L at track T-junction in Malham at 2.2m/3.5km and turning R on C-road at 2.3m/3.7km into Malham and the start at 2.6m/4.1km.

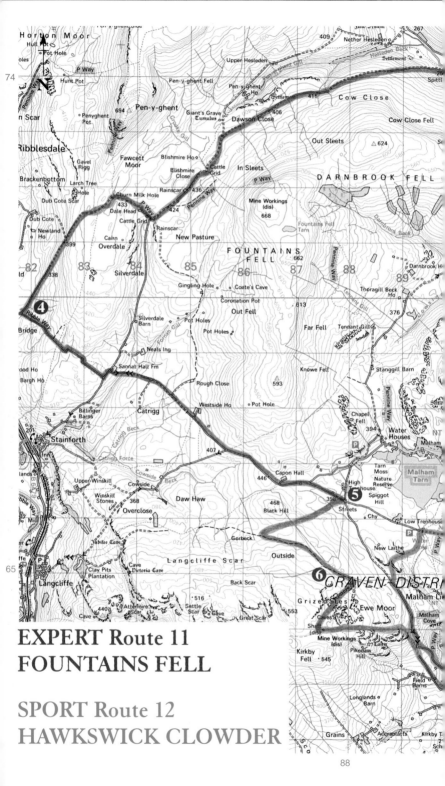

EXPERT Route 11
FOUNTAINS FELL

SPORT Route 12
HAWKSWICK CLOWDER

88

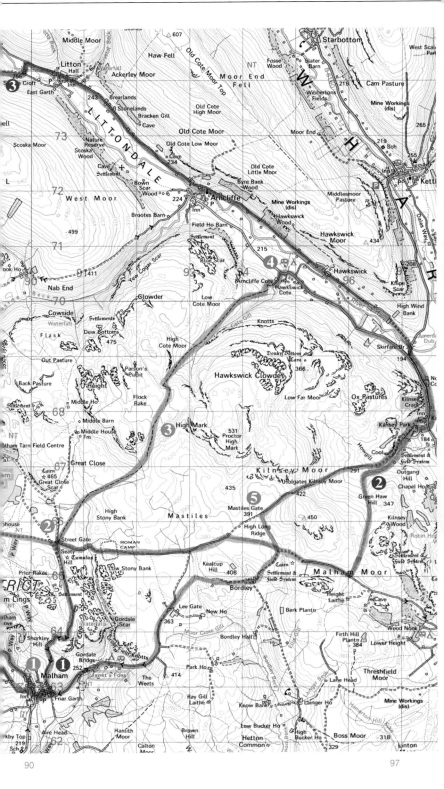

SPORT Route 12
HAWKSWICK CLOWDER

DISTANCE
16 miles (26km)
HEIGHT-GAIN
2350ft (710m)
TIME
2.5hrs(dry)
3.5hrs (wet)
NAVIGATION
SKILLS
moderate
RIDE DIRECTION
clockwise

A tad tough for new-comers but the tech-nical quotient's low; the scenics sumptuous.

The Malham valley makes a stunning backdrop as you climb up to Street Gate to pick up the unclassified track to Arncliffe Cote (this road may be down-graded to bridleway in the future). In the mist navigation can be a bit tricky in places but follow the directions carefully and you'll be OK. If it's clear, Wharfedale's amazing limestone crags come into view as you crest Flock Rake then it's the twisting, mostly grass, descent to Arncote to enjoy – slippery when wet.

The return leg to Malham makes use of another ancient road – Mastiles Lane. It was surfaced all the way but recent adoption by powered vehicles has churned the top-most section to quagmire. This loop avoids the gloop but it's still testing. The last haul up over Kilnsey Moor is a physically demanding and mentally intimidating climb – more so when those limestone 'cobbles' have a lick of water on them. Watch your speed on the drive into Bordley and again on the lanes to Malham. If you've time take a look at Gordale Scar – it's an astonishing sight.

❶ Start Malham Bridge (GR901629). From the Buck Inn head NNW (towards Settle and Stainforth), forking R on signed bridleway track (just over cattle grid) at 1.7m/2.7km, turning R (ENE) through gate at 1.9m/3km, soon swinging L and turning R on C-road (by Malham Tarn) at 2.4m/3.8km to go SO X-roads with unclassified county tracks to Street Gate at 3.2m/5.1km.

❷ Go through gate, immediately forking L (NNE, onto High Cote Lane unclassified county track), swinging L (N) and going through gate at 0.5m/0.8km (up Gordale Beck at first), turning R (E, green track vague at first) at 0.7m/1.15km and up through gate at 1.5m/2.4km. Swing L (NNE), down through gate at 0.12m/0.2km, over High Mark col, keeping R (NE) by waymarker to go through gate at 0.6m/1km.

❸ Swing L (NE, keeping alongside broken wall then through another gate), turning L by waymarker at 0.4m/0.6km, soon swinging R (NE) down through gate at 0.7m/1.15km, going through ford/gate/ford combo at 1.12m/1.8km, swinging L (NNE then ENE down spur) after next gate and through hairpin bends to another gate at 2.3m/3.7km. Go through gate, SO (past Arncliffe Cote farm; take extra care; this RoW is under threat) to T-junction with C-road at 0.2m/0.3km.

❹ Turn R, keeping R on to B6160 at 1.9m/3km, turning R at T-junc-tion (just past The Tennant Arms, Kilnsey) at 2.6m/4.1km and forking L at signposted T-junction (Mastiles Lane track) at 3m/4.8km over Kilnsey Moor to Mastiles Gate T-junction at 4.8m/7.75km.

❺ Turn L, going SO gated X-roads at 0.5m/0.8km, zigzagging R/L through Bordley Green Farm (approach is steep, please ride slow) at 1.5m/2.4km on obvious bridle-way track that swings R (across field corner) to go through gate at 1.5m/2.4km. Zigzag R/L (across lit-tle valley), turning R at Lee Gate farm gate at 0.6m/0.9km, turning L at T-junction at 0.6m/1km, soon joining C-road (nearby Gordale Scar and Janet's Foss waterfall are worth detours) and going SO at T-junction above Malham at 2.9m/4.6km down to start at 3.15m/5km.

SPORT Route 13
LANGCLIFFE SCAR

DISTANCE
14 miles (22km)
HEIGHT-GAIN
2160ft (655m)
TIME
2.5hrs (dry)
3.5hrs (wet)
NAVIGATION
SKILLS
moderate
RIDE DIRECTION
either way

Slippery when wet, it's a slick rock limestone loop with 800ft (250m) of gravity-suck to close the circuit

Malham's a pretty place but all the moorland routes are up. 1000ft (300m) of up. Happily, half that's on tarmac and that gives a good view of the spectacular Cove cliffs. The descent to Stockdale is an interesting exercise in "skip 'n slip" when wet – and it usually is – then it's a mix of tarmac and muddy track all the way into Settle. Followed by a rocky climb to fields where clay singletrack contours its way past Clay Pits Plantation to the road. But we touch tarmac only briefly. Onwards and upwards on ancient byway that, before too long, goes in for some big-time bog-trotting. Negotiating this road's dark, peaty pools is a lottery. One barely wets your tread, the next immediately engulfs the front wheel and it's endo time! If it's dry it's a doddle. After that, the run down to Malham is pure fun.

❶ Start Malham Bridge (GR901629). From the Buck Inn head NNW (towards Settle and Stainforth), turning L at gate with bridleway signpost at 1m/1.6km (up gated, zigzag track), past footpath signpost and over Kirkby Fell col to join Stockdale farm drive through gate at 3.6m/5.8km. Turn right, turning R at C-road T-junction at 1.3m/2.1km, turning L onto bridleway track at 1.4m/2.2km (past Blacks Plantation onto tarmac road) and keeping right at the next two T-junctions to T-junction with C-road at 2.7m/4.3km.

❷ Turn L (skirting Settle), keeping R at all T-junctions to T-junction with unclassified county track at 0.5m/0.8km. Fork R (up track then contouring in field, between walls again and out alongside field boundary), going through gate at 0.75m/1.2km, immediately swinging R (faint grass singletrack becomes obvious after 220yds/200m) on gated singletrack past woods to gate onto C-road at 1.3m/2.1km.

❸ Turn R, keeping R up unclassified county road soon after, past Victoria Caves, over col (when gravel gives way to grass), crossing stream at 1.9m/3km, swinging R (on boggy moorland track around Gorbeck) up to two gates at 3.6m/5.75km. Go through RH gate (down gated track), turning R on C-road at 1m/1.6km, going SO through gate on LH bend at 1.8m/2.9km (on faint bridleway across field at first then on walled lane), turning L at track T-junction in Malham at 3.15m/5km and turning R on C-road at 3.25m/5.2km into Malham and the start at 3.5m/5.6km.

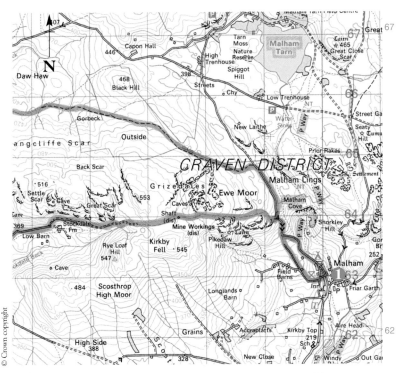

LOWER WHARFEDALE

An evening saunter above Skyreholme, Wharfedale (Route 16)

EXPERT Route 14
HETTON AND BARDEN MOORS

DISTANCE
32 miles (51km)
HEIGHT-GAIN
3355ft (1015m)
TIME
4.5hrs (dry)
5.5hrs (wet)
NAVIGATION
SKILLS
easy/moderate
RIDE DIRECTION
anticlockwise

A pot-pourri of Dale trails – a delight to ride whatever the weather with a four mile descent to endure (Not!)

A nice tarmac warm-up on the Wharfedale road before cutting to granny-cog on the climb over Threshfield Moor. But if you thought that track was a technical teaser then be prepared for the bog-snatchers that follow. They've been known to swallow a quad bike! A touch of green lane at Height Laithe, bounded by a medley of crumbling walls and neat stone barn, is a summary of the Dales condensed into an acre of landscape.

Beyond Bordley white tracks cut across deep, green pastures where we join the lane to Lee Gate for a short interlude of tyre-hum then it's back to track (easy to overshoot the junction) for the climb onto The Weets. Grassy singletrack dips down to the head of Winterburn Reservoir but its benign nature hides a few drop-ins – or 'fly-outs' if you prefer! The neat little bridge marks the start of a short, sharp technical climb that delivers you to the top of the big-ring run down to Hetton. Hetton Beck's spanned by a bizarre stone – as in one big rock – bridge that looks distinctly second-hand.

Beware the traffic on the B6265 – more quarry lorries. Rylstone Ridge, its craggy cliffs topped by a gaunt cross, lies ahead and marks the last big climb of the day. The old bridleway follows twisting singletrack but the new one may well follow the less testing shooting track. Hard work all the same! Out on the top it's a sea-change from limestone and lush pastures to gritstone and grouse moor. An all too short section of techno-track is cut off in its prime with path erosion control. Underneath lurks mega-bog so it's not as bad as it seems. Then as sweeping vistas over Embsay Moor open up the track takes a downward trend. For miles. All big-ring spinning as you high-tail it for the road at Halton Height. Shooting track gives way to green bridleway over Middle Hare Head – beware the bog as you drop off the hill, into the woods for some sinuous single-tracking through the trees and off down to Bolton's Pavilion for a well-earned cuppa. (The private road through the valley here has permissive access for cyclists using this guide book.)

❶ Start New Inn (ask in pub about secure parking) in Appletreewick (GR 052601). Turn R (towards Burnsall), turning R onto B6160 immediately after Burnsall Bridge at 1.5m/2.4km, forking L off B-road at 4.7m/7.5km into Threshfield to T-junction with B6265 at 4.9m/7.8km. Turn L, turning R (busy road; care!) at T-junction with unclassified road at 0.2m/0.3km, keeping SO at T-junction at 0.7m/1.15km to gate on to Threshfield Moor at 1m/1.6km.

❷ Turn R, keeping L at T-junctions at 0.1m/0.15km and 0.4m/0.6km and by waymarker at 1m/1.6km (on to singletrack bridleway) and turning R at T-junction with waymarker at 1.25m/2km (on to track) to gate on to Malham Moor at 1.9m/3km. Go SO (boggy singletrack with marker posts), swinging R at 0.3m/0.5km and passing barns at Height Laithe to C-road at 0.8m/1.3km.

❸ Turn L, turning L at gated X-roads at 0.9m/1.4km, zigzagging R/L through Bordley Green Farm (approach is steep, please ride slow) at 1.4m/2.2km on obvious bridleway track that swings R (across field corner) to go through gate at 2m/3.2km. Zigzag R/L (across little valley), turning R at Lee Gate farm gate at 0.6m/0.9km, turning L at T-junction at 0.6m/1km and soon joining C-road to T-junction with bridleway track (easy to miss; just over brow of hill signpost obscured by wall) at 1.25m/2km.

❹ Turn L (signed Calton), keeping L (signed Hetton) at bridleway T-junction (near trig point on The Weets) at 0.3m/0.5km, swinging R (round hill top) after gate at 0.6m/1km and turning R at gate at 1.5m/2.4km to bridge above Winterburn Reservoir at 2.4m/3.9km. Cross bridge, immediately up L/R/L zigzag (effectively SO) and going SO gated bridleway X-roads at 0.5m/0.8km to T-junction with C-road in Hetton at 1.9m/3km.

❺ Turn R, turning L onto bridleway track at 0.15m/0.25km, joining drive at 0.5m/0.8km, turning R at T-junction with C-road at 0.6m/1km (immediately under railway) to T-junction with B6265 in Rylstone (busy road, take care) at 0.8m/1.3km. Turn R, turning L onto bridleway track at 0.25m/0.4km to gated bridleway T-junction at 0.75m/1.2km.

❻ NOTE: Next bit of singletrack bridleway is tricky to follow and is destined to be re-routed onto track 100yds/90m N. For now turn L through gate, turning R (on 'track') at 100yds, turning L (up singletrack) at 2nd telegraph pole at 0.15m/0.25km, passing just to R of trees, turning R at T-junction with track at 0.5m/0.8km and going SO through gate at 0.6m/1km to gate onto Embsay Moor at 0.8m/1.3km. Go SO (random blue spots mark the route), passing through wall at 0.12m/0.2km, joining track at T-junction at 1m/1.6km, keeping R at T-junction at 1.7m/2.7km (100yds beyond waymarker on Brown Bank) and forking R (ESE, easy to miss) at T-junction with singletrack at 3.6m/5.8km to C-road at Halton Moor at 3.9m/6.3km.

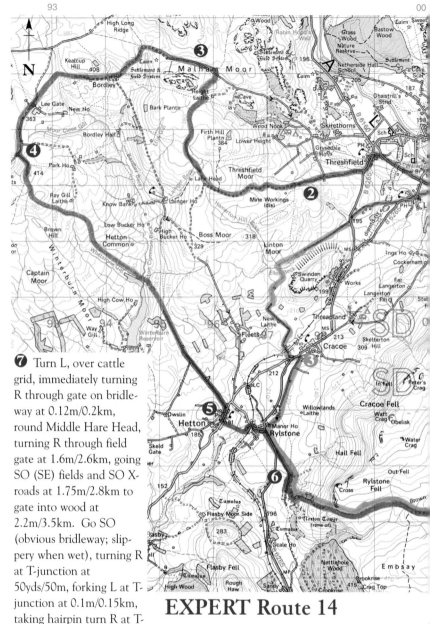

7 Turn L, over cattle grid, immediately turning R through gate on bridleway at 0.12m/0.2km, round Middle Hare Head, turning R through field gate at 1.6m/2.6km, going SO (SE) fields and SO X-roads at 1.75m/2.8km to gate into wood at 2.2m/3.5km. Go SO (obvious bridleway; slippery when wet), turning R at T-junction at 50yds/50m, forking L at T-junction at 0.1m/0.15km, taking hairpin turn R at T-junction at 0.3m/0.5km and exit woods to pair of gates at 0.5m/0.8km. Go through LH gate and swing R to join track at 0.15m/0.25km down to B6160 in Bolton Abbey at 0.25m/0.4km.

EXPERT Route 14
HETTON AND BARDEN

SPORT Route 15
CRACOE FELL

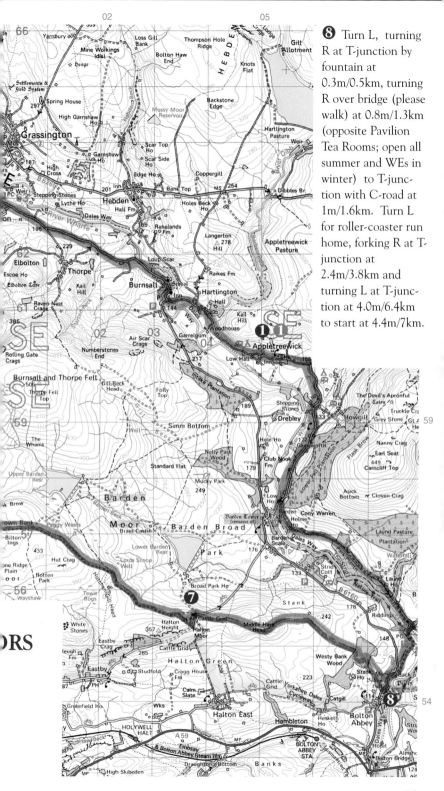

8 Turn L, turning R at T-junction by fountain at 0.3m/0.5km, turning R over bridge (please walk) at 0.8m/1.3km (opposite Pavilion Tea Rooms; open all summer and WEs in winter) to T-junction with C-road at 1m/1.6km. Turn L for roller-coaster run home, forking R at T-junction at 2.4m/3.8km and turning L at T-junction at 4.0m/6.4km to start at 4.4m/7km.

SPORT Route 15
CRACOE FELL

DISTANCE
22 miles (35km)
HEIGHT-GAIN
1700ft (515m)
TIME
3hrs (dry)
3.5hrs (wet)
NAVIGATION
SKILLS
easy
RIDE DIRECTION
either way

Ideal winter's after-noon out with the option of a tea stop at weekends

Essentially a short-cut option on the longer Route 14, this loop is a brilliant ride for those with limited experience but eager to exercise their new-won skills. Just be sure to follow the route directions as you make your way through Linton Moor.

❶ Start New Inn (ask in pub about secure parking) in Appletreewick (GR 052601). Turn R (towards Burnsall), turning R onto B6160 immediately after Burnsall Bridge at 1.5m/2.4km, forking L off B-road (towards Linton) at T-junction at 3.9m/6.3km and forking L onto B6265 soon after to T-junction with bridleway track at 4.5m/7.2km (just after Linton).

❷ Fork R, dropping down to go SO bridleway X-roads with B6265 (busy road!) at 0.7m/1.15km, turning L (S) at bridleway T-junction at 1.7m/2.75km (vague), immediately through ford, passing to L of trees, (don't go through gate at 1.9m/3.1km) across fields and keeping R of barn to gate in field corner at 2.1m/3.4km. Go SO (on track) to track/road X-roads near Cracoe at 0.8m/1.3km.

❸ Turn L (towards Cracoe), turning R (care – busy road!) onto bridleway track at 0.1m/0.15km, keeping L at T-junction at 0.7m/1.15km and keeping L around farm and church to T-junction with B6265 in Rylstone at 1.1m/1.75km. Turn L, turning L at T-junction with bridleway track at 0.25m/0.4km to bridleway gate at 0.75m/1.2km. Follow Expert Route 14 from para No 6.

FUN Route 16
APPLETREEWICK PASTURE

Always a delight to ride, this little loop kicks off with tarmac to stretch those city-stiff legs before tackling the only climb up onto Eller Edge. The Eller Edge leg (optional I guess) is well worth doing – especially if you're an up-and-coming descender but watch out for the rut and rubble when you return. On the final descent from Appletreewick Pasture beware of those grass chicanes – in the wet they're slippery!

DISTANCE
9.5 miles (15km)
HEIGHT-GAIN
900ft (275m)
TIME
1hr (dry)
1.5hrs (wet)
NAVIGATION SKILLS
easy
RIDE DIRECTION
anticlockwise

Sweet little intro to Dale trails; a pub-to-pub evening saunter with scenics to savour. Made-to-measure night ride.

❶ Start New Inn (ask in pub about secure parking) in Appletreewick (GR 052601). Turn L (uphill), keeping SO at T-junction at 0.5m/0.8km, forking R (towards Parcevall Hall Gdns) at T-junction at 0.7m/1.15km and turning R at T-junction at 1.25m/2km to track T-junction at 2.1m/3.3km.

❷ Turn R up to gate at Eller Edge Nook at 0.8m/1.3km (take in views), returning to turn R at T-junction to B6265 at Dry Gill at 2.8m/4.5km. Turn L, turning L off B-road at 1st T-junction, turning R through gate onto bridleway track at 1.75m/ 2.8km (just after LH bend; beware of farm stock) and keeping SO at T-junction at 2.7m/4.3km to gated T-junction by buildings at 2.9m/4.6km.

❸ Turn R (grassy trail turns rubbly; watch out for walkers) turning L on to C-road at 0.6m/0.9km back to start at 1.5m/2.4km.

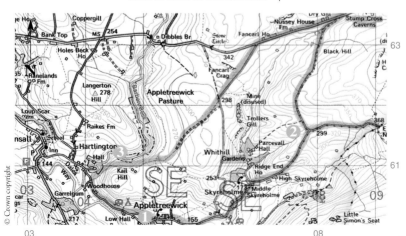

© Crown copyright

COVERDALE

Tricky dip on the roller-coaster path around Little Whernside (Route 17)

EXPERT Route 17
THE WHERNSIDES

DISTANCE
25m (40km)
HEIGHT-GAIN
3800ft (1150m)
TIME
6.5hrs (dry)
9hrs (wet)
NAVIGATION
SKILLS
moderate/difficult
RIDE DIRECTION
clockwise (dry) anti-
clockwise (wet)

*A full day out on the
fells – not for the
faint-hearted. It's gru-
elling in the wet so
wait for a dry spell
before tackling this
scenic roller-coaster.*

The climb over the Whernsides is sodden singletrack so if it's wet take the track over Arkleside
instead. Even in the dry adverse gradient, tussock
grass and gloop will reduce all but the toughest
riders to jelly. And the map's a tad optimistic
when it classes the decreasing contour values to
Coverdale Head as 'downhill' – the muddy path
plummets into boggy ravines at regular intervals
so the granny ring rules.

From Coverdale the route contour trots above
Wharfedale – the views are sumptuous, the track
entertaining. A stiff climb – a push most likely
unless it's exceptionally dry – over the shoulders of
Buckden Pike then the bridleway plunges down
steep, sometimes boggy, singletrack to Walden
Head. The area's peppered with grass-covered
grykes so watch out and there's a hidden step right
on the lip of the last, steep drop. From the fords –
two becks converge here – a new bridleway route
may be in place; follow YDNP signs to pick up the
lane.

The climb up from Cote is a killer. The gradient
increases as you go and just as the track kinks ruts
are added to the traction testing sea of loose rock.
The gate doesn't come soon enough! After the
gully's been negotiated it's over the top and a can-
ter down to Coverdale with more random rubble
on the final bit of track. A short sojourn on lane
then back to track for the last uphill struggle of the
day topped off by a short, sharp drop back to Scar
– watch out for the rut 'n rubble though!

❶ Start Scar House Resv Car Park
(GR069766). Turn L (towards dam),
turning R over dam, then L on track
to T-junction by sheepfolds at
1.7m/2.7km. NOTE: If ground conditions are wet turn R here and follow
track for 2.5m/4km over to C-road at
Arkleside in Coverdale then turn L for
4.75m/7.6km up to signed T-junction

with bridleway. Fork R (SW) and follow directions from para No 3 below.

❷ Fork L (immediately through gap in wall), going through gate at 0.5m/0.8km (on to roughly contouring singletrack with marker posts), swinging R (NW) by marker post at 2.4m/3.8km and turning L (SW, by wall) at 2.5m/4km to go through gate with waymarker at 2.75m/4.4km. Keep L (WSW, by marker post), through boggy gullies, descending R at 1.1m/1.7km, going through gate and turning R on C-road at Coverdale Head at 1.6m/2.5km to signed T-junction with bridleway at 1.9m/3km.

❸ Take hairpin turn L (SW, on bridleway track), swinging R through gate at 0.8m/1.3km, up gully and forking R (towards Starbotton) at signed bridleway T-junction at 1.5m/2.4km to bridleway T-junction immediately after gate at 1.75m/2.8km. Turn R, going through gate at 0.2m/0.3km, keeping L alongside wall and rejoining track at 0.75m/1.2km to bridleway T-junction at 1.4m/2.2km (by cairn on Starbotton Fell).

❹ Turn R (up and past ruin at 0.25m/0.4km), going SO through gate at 0.5m/0.8km (below

Buckden Pike), through spoil heaps, swinging R (NE) at 1.2m/1.9km (boggy!) down to stream confluence below Walden Moor at 2.3m/3.7km. Cross RH beck. Keep SO (NNE, on signed singletrack bridleway) close by Walden Beck, swinging R at 0.5m/0.8km (where bridleway squeezes between wall and beck) and passing by Kentucky House on to C-road at 0.8m/1.3km. Keep R (NE), taking hairpin turn R at 4.0m/6.4km to T-junction with bridleway at Cote at 4.5m/7.2km.

❺ Turn L, swinging R immediately after gate at 0.25m/0.4km, keeping L (SSE, up valley) at T-junction at 0.4m/0.6km, swinging L (E, away from wall) at 1.5m/2.4km, zigzagging L/R (effectively SO, through ford) at 1.75m/2.8km and keeping L at T-junction at 2.8m/4.5km to T-junction with C-road at Carlton at 3.0m/4.8km. Turn R (towards Horsehouse), turning L (towards Arkleside) at T-junction with unclassified road at 2.75m/4.4km to gated track at 3.1m/5km. Climb SO, keeping R at T-junction at 0.75m/1.2km (care! rough descent) and turning L at familiar T-junction at 2.2m/3.5km onto outbound route (careful on rubbly drop to dam) to start at 4m/6.4km.

EXPERT Route 17
THE WHERNSIDES

FUN Route 18
COVERDALE

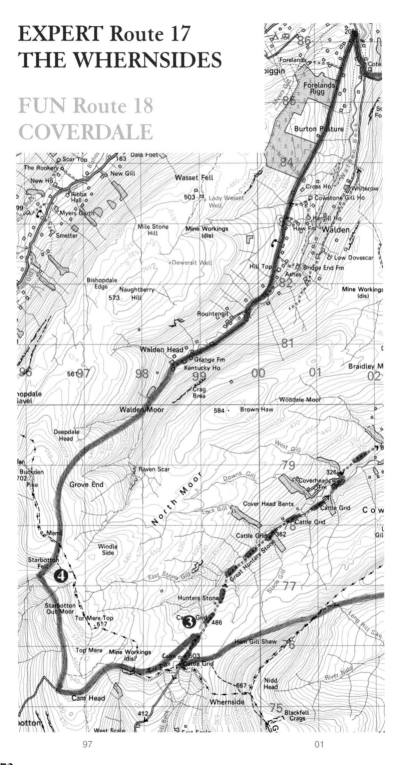

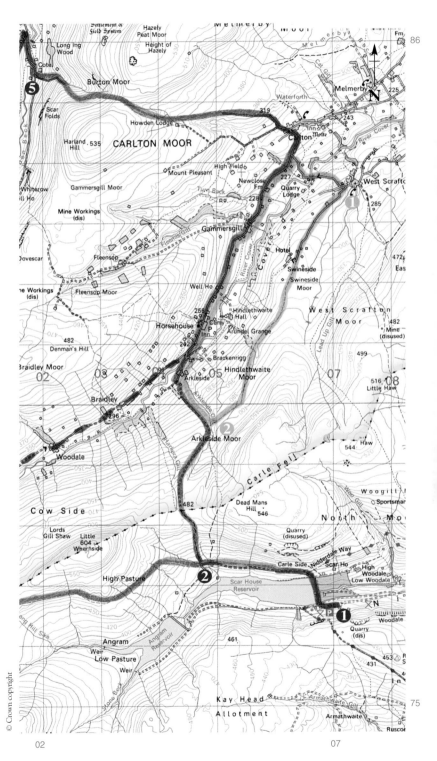

FUN Route 18
COVERDALE

DISTANCE
8 miles (13km)
HEIGHT-GAIN
860ft (260m)
TIME
1.5hrs (dry)
2hrs (wet)
NAVIGATION
SKILLS
easy/moderate
RIDE DIRECTION
anticlockwise

Excellent pot-pourri of lane, track and singletrack with a taste of open fell riding. Ideal for the adventurous tyro.

The climb up from Arkelside's when the work begins but it's soon over. There's a couple of awesome little chasms to cross, the first right after you quit the track. Watch your footing. The next, after a spot of open moor, is rideable if you're experienced.

❶ Start West Scrafton (GR074836). From telephone box head (SW) towards Carlton on C-road, turning L (towards Horsehouse and Arkleside) at T-junction at 0.9m/1.4km and turning L (towards Arkleside) at T-junction with unclassified road at 3.3m/5.3km and joining gated track to T-junction with single-track bridleway immediately after gate at 4.2m/6.7km.

❷ Turn L (across ravine), swinging L (NNE) after gate at 0.5m/0.8km (following marker posts), passing signpost near plantation at 1m/1.6km, almost immediately zigzagging R/L through ravine, going SO (NE) track X-roads onto singletrack at 1.25m/2km and swinging L (NNE then N) at 1.6m/2.6km to T-junction with bridleway drive at Swineside at 2.25m/3.6km. Go SO, going SO at T-junction with C-road at 1m/1.6km to start at 1.1m/1.8km.

NIDDERDALE

Rock-strewn descent to Scar House Reservoir, Nidderdale (Route 19)

SPORT Route 19
NIDDERDALE

DISTANCE
22 miles (36km)
HEIGHT-GAIN
2400ft (730m)
TIME
3hrs (dry)
3.5hrs (wet)
NAVIGATION
SKILLS
easy/moderate
RIDE DIRECTION
clockwise

An all-weather circuit complete with tricky drops, testing climbs, a soupçon of singletrack and sea-sized puddles.

Like all good off-road routes the big climbs are on tarmac. Up to Middlesmoor is the first, but before that be prepared for a couple of gates on the farm track from Ramsgill. Middlesmoor marks a welcome return to track – track that sports a semi-technical climb quickly followed by a switchback, stone-ridden descent to Scar with a ravine slotted in somewhere along the way. Brilliant! It's a flat dash across the dam then a cobbly climb up onto North Moor – with views over Nidderdale for company and a radical ravine to up the interest factor. A weaving line, climbing along the sides is the only way out of that one! If it's wet, mega-puddles make an appearance after Jordan Moss – ideal splash 'n dash territory – with the ride's technical quotient wrapped up down rough track into the Dale.

❶ Start Pateley Bridge long-stay car park (GR158655). Return to B6265 in town centre and turn L, turning R at 0.2m/0.3km (just after bridge) and forking L by Ramsgill village green at 2.8m/4.5km (onto farm track; watch out for gate on bend at 4.6m/7.4km) to T-junction with C-road by bridge at 5.1m/8.2km.

❷ Turn R over bridge, turning L (towards Middlesmoor) at next T-junction, joining track at 1m/1.6km, keeping SO at T-junctions at 1.1m/1.8km and at 1.3m/2.1km and down rough descent to track T-junction at Scar House Resv at 3.15m/5km. Turn R, turning L over dam, forking L at T-junction at 0.5m/0.8km, turning R at T-junction at 0.6m/1km and going SO track X-roads at 0.7m/1.1km to track/singletrack bridleway T-junction (easy to miss; it's by drainage runnel 140yds/125m after bridge) at 1.7m/2.7km.

❸ Fork L (NNE then NNW, up vague singletrack), turning R at indistinct singletrack X-roads at 0.2m/0.3km (onto contouring singletrack on Woogill Moor), passing mine shaft at 0.6m/0.9km to gated track junction at

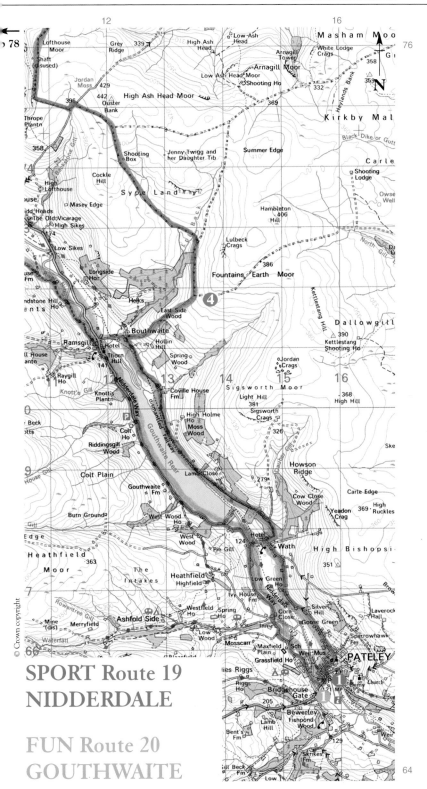

SPORT Route 19
NIDDERDALE

FUN Route 20
GOUTHWAITE

0.7m/1.1km. Go SO through gate, going SO at X-roads at 1.9m/3km and swinging L at 3m/4.8km to gated T-junction with C-road at 3.3m/5.3km. Turn L, almost immediately turning R (signed Unsuitable For Motors) at next T-junction, forking R at T-junction at 0.5m/0.8km, keeping R at T-junction at 2.2m/3.5km to unclassified track T-junction at 2.75m/4.4km

(just beyond Lul Beck bridge).

❹ Turn R (down on gated track), turning L at T-junction at 1m/1.6km in Bouthwaite (alongside Gouthwaite Resv; note spectacular filled quarry at 2.4m/3.8km), turning L at T-junction at 2.8m/4.5km, keeping SO (towards Pateley Bridge) at all T-junctions to X-roads with B6265 in Pateley Bridge at 4.6m/7.4km. Go SO to start.

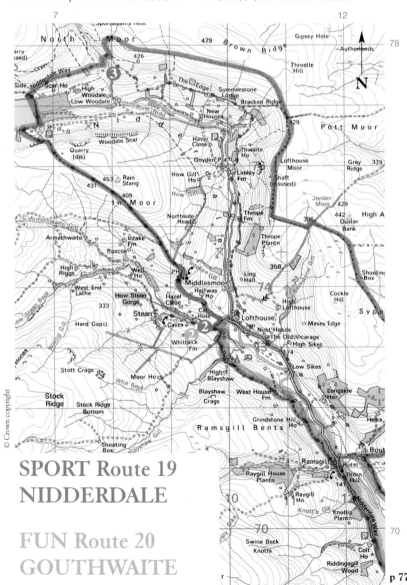

SPORT Route 19
NIDDERDALE

FUN Route 20
GOUTHWAITE

p 77

FUN Route 20
GOUTHWAITE

Ramsgill marks the start of the off-road – farm track for the most part with nothing more serious than a bit of mud to cope with – apart from a surprise gate below Blayshaw – speed freaks beware – and a short, sharp, cobbled drop that follows soon after. The track alongside Gouthwaite is easy riding but don't forget to take a look at the old quarry just before you get to Wath.

DISTANCE
12 miles (20km)
HEIGHT-GAIN
630ft (190m)
TIME
1hr (dry)
1.5hrs (wet)
NAVIGATION SKILLS
easy
RIDE DIRECTION
either way

Nidderdale escaped being included in the National Park despite being one of the prettiest valleys. This loop's at lake shore level most of the time so don't expect anything exerting.

❶ Start Pateley Bridge long-stay car park (GR158655). Return to B6265 in town centre and turn L, turning R at 0.2m/0.3km (just after bridge) and forking L by Ramsgill village green at 2.8m/4.5km (onto farm track; watch out for gate on bend at 4.6m/7.4km) to T-junction with C-road by bridge at 5.1m/8.2km.

❷ Turn R over bridge, keeping R at next T-junction, keeping R (towards Pateley) at T-junction in Lofthouse at 0.4m/0.6km and turning L at T-junction at 2.2m/3.5km (just before Ramsgill bridge) to T-junction with tracks in Bouthwaite at 2.4m/3.9km. Turn R (alongside Gouthwaite Resv; note spectacular filled quarry at 0.8m/1.3km), turning L at T-junction at 1.2m/1.9km, keeping SO (towards Pateley Bridge) at all T-junctions to X-roads with B6265 in Pateley Bridge at 4m/6.4km. Go SO to start.

DENTDALE

Slick-rock singletrack on Twistleton Scars, Whernside (Route 21)

EXPERT Route 21
WHERNSIDE WANDER

DISTANCE
23 miles (37km)
HEIGHT-GAIN
2650ft (805m)
TIME
4.5hrs (dry)
6.5hrs (wet)
NAVIGATION
SKILLS
moderate
RIDE DIRECTION
either way

One of the Dales' most scenic circuits that dials in bone-cracking technical trail and dishes out dirt on the final run to Dent; even the skilled will thrill to an 'unctuous' moment or two. This loop is big, tough and technical - all rideable on a good day - but with few 'opt-outs' available it's an all-or-nothing outing.

Chapel-le-Dale's an optional start if you're domiciled south and east of the Dales; otherwise Dent is the obvious choice but both lie at the end of some excellent, offroad frolics. A couple of miles of lane take you to the Dales Way where it struggles over Great Wold. One of Yorkshire's titanic track ascents, it is by far the hardest on this loop. On top, contouring peat path gets a dressing of grit where it flies down Force Gill Ridge. Watch out for the bends at the bottom and don't lose the back end or you'll be off for a short flight! Shattered rock and random rubble turn up the technical edge before a maze of farm tracks across sheep-stocked meadows take you towards Twistleton Scars. Navigation's not a problem. Just follow the signs for Scar End.

Twistleton Scars: acres of rippling, contorted limestone laid bare in levels that stretch out from under Whernside — one of the Dales' most prominent ridges. Stark even in summer, the limestone landscape's almost lunar. But beware. The twisting, kick-back and rock bedecked bridleway should have a warning sign "SLIPPERY WHEN WET". Even in mist this stuff's deadly. And all ends with a rocky drop off Ewes Top which is best described as trials terrain! After all that a detour to see Thornton Force — a scenic wonder — makes for a welcome rest.

Tarmac and broken track take you up Kingsdale and over High Pike hill to what's left of Green Lane. Now that 4x4s have created a corrugated mire mixed with top-stones, stop-rocks and murky ribbons of water it's tough going but still rideable. Just! But you'll lose all that angst and rebuild the positive trail vibes on the rut and rubble ride back down to Dent.

❶ Start Dent car-park (GR704871, toilets here). Turn left (SSE), forking right at next T-junction and swinging L at next (in village still), turning R up

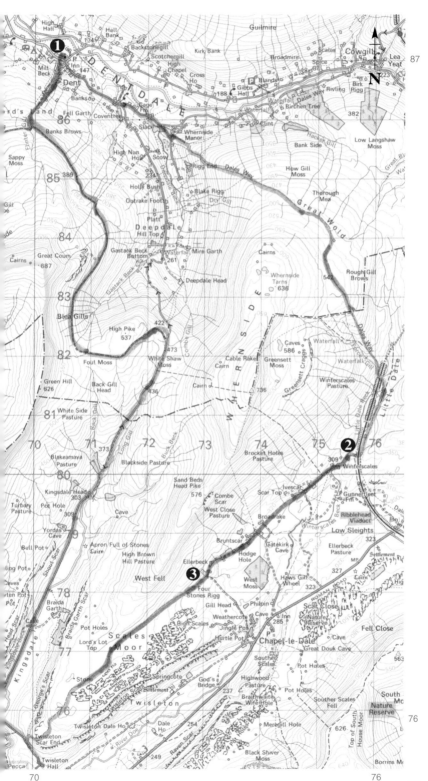

dead-end at 1.4m/2.25km, taking hairpin turn L up bridleway (signed Craven Way) at 1.6m/2.5km, swinging L through boggy bit at 4m/6.4km and turning R at T-junction at 6.6m/ 10.5km under railway to gate.

❷ Go through gate, turning L on tarmac at Winterscales Farm at 0.3m/0.5km, keeping R at T-junction at 0.4m/0.6km (now follow bridleway signed Scar End), going SO at T-junction on grass track at 0.8m/1.25km, forking R on singletrack at 1m/1.6km and through bridle-gate at 1.1m/1.7km to gate below barn at 1.5m/2.4km.

❸ Go through gate, immediately SO staggered X-roads, going SO on bridleway singletrack at T-junction soon after Ellerbeck Farm at 0.5m/0.8km (access point from Chapel-le-Dale start), forking R to follow marker posts at 2m/3.2km, turning L at cliff edge at 3.75m/6km then turning R down by wall soon after and turning R on track at 3.9m/6.3km to C-road in Kingsdale at 4.7m/7.5km.

❹ Turn R, turning L up bridleway track at 4.6m/7.3km (very rutted, gloopy when wet), swinging L at gated T-junction at 7.8m/ 12.5km, turning R at T-junction (signed Dent) at 9.0m/14.5km and going SO at all junctions through Dent to start at 9.9m/15.8km.

HOWGILL FELLS

Cutting a splash in Chapel Beck Ford, Howgill Fells (Route 22)

EXPERT Route 22
RAVENSTONEDALE COMMON

DISTANCE
26 miles (42km)
HEIGHT-GAIN
4250ft (1285m)
TIME
6hrs (dry)
7hrs (wet)
NAVIGATION
SKILLS
moderate/
difficult
RIDE DIRECTION
anticlockwise (dry),
clockwise (wet)

A rough 'n tough route with rich rewards, Ravenstonedale Common is a radical ride and topping out at 2211ft (670m) gives it the biggest climb total in the book!

This ride's for the fittest only – once you've kicked those cranks you're committed to the full Monty. In winter ride it clockwise – that way there are plenty of opportunities to drop onto the road if you run out of light or time after Ravenstonedale. The significant features of this loop are the miles of technical singletrack through Bowderdale and the seriously steep spur off White Fell. Both need a high level of skill and strength to ride. For the adventurous few the hard-won prizes are stunning panoramas from the Howgill peaks and pitting your wits against a testing trail.

It's a good idea to take ten at Rams Gill ford, near the head of Bowderdale, before climbing Hare Shaw, and watch out for the spectacular scenery over Cautley Spout (on your left). On top it's easy to head for the trig – don't; there's no Right of Way and the Commoners' Association is highly sensitive to the erosion caused by trespassers. Last, but by no means least, the descent off White Fell is precipitous. Don't be deceived by the lack of rock 'n ruts and let it rip – the top's really slippery if it's at all damp and if you hit the twisty track off the bottom of the spur at speed you'll be in trouble. So will walkers coming the other way!

Unlike other loops in this book ride direction really is dictated by ground conditions – don't ride it anticlockwise if it's really wet. Navigation clockwise is pretty straightforward but points to watch for are:

Chapel Beck Ford – after crossing keep L up track then keep R on track then grass singletrack up White Fell spur.

White Fell Head – aim for trig on The Calf then fork L onto minor singletrack about 0.15m/0.25km short of it.

Great Force Gill Rigg Tarn – fork R onto descent just after tarn.

Weasdale – there's a gate on the bridge so slow down and remember to fork R at the T-junction 0.8m/1.3km after that.

Ravenstonedale – leave on the road signed Adamthwaite.

Cautley Beck – after crossing footbridge keep beside boundary wall for 0.5m/0.8km then go through gate into fields.

❶ Start Sedbergh car park (GR659922) (Toilets here). Exit car park and turn L (E, on main street) keeping L (on A684) at T-junction at 110yds/100m, keeping L (onto A683 towards Kirkby Stephen) at T-junction at 0.25m/0.4km and forking L at T-junction with unclassified road at 0.8m/1.3km (steep dip and bend at 2.1m/3.4km) to Fawcett Bank farm at 2.2m/3.5km. Keep SO on roughly contouring bridleway singletrack, forking R (NNE) across fields on vague singletrack at 1.1m/1.8km and forking L (N) through gate onto moor at 1.5m/2.4km to ford Cautley Holme Beck at 2m/3.2km just downstream of twin-pole foot-bridge.

❷ Swing R (NE, on vague bridle-way singletrack at first), keeping L at bridleway T-junction at 0.12m/0.2km and taking hairpin turn R across Backside Beck ford to Narthwaite farm at 0.9m/1.4km. Turn L in yard then immediately forking R up by wall (steep and rubbly at first then along muddy, roughly contouring bridleway trail), track starts at 1.3m/2.1km, to Adamthwaite Farm at 1.75m/2.8km. Keep R onto C-road (steep zigzag at 0.7m/1.15km, take it slow!), turning R at T-junction at 2.6m/4.2km and keeping L at next T-junction to T-junction in Ravenstonedale at 3m/4.8km.

❸ Turn L, keeping L at T-junction at 0.1m/0.15km, turning L at T-junction with old A685, over bridge and turning L at next T-junction to T-junction with gated bridleway at 0.6m/1km (1st gate on R, 100yds/100m from main road). Turn R through gate onto gated bridleway, alongside wall, joining green lane for a time, keeping L (SW) through gate at 0.5m/0.8km, keeping by fence and then heading SO (SW) field to gap in field wall at 0.6m/1km. Go SO down rough track, swinging R at 0.1m/0.15km then through gates to T-junction with unclassi-fied road at 0.25m/ 0.4km. Turn L, keeping L at T-junction with C-road at 0.4m/0.6km, turning L at T-junction with bridleway/unclas-sified road in Weasdale at 1m/1.6km, keeping R at 1.2m/1.9km, joining muddy track at 1.3m/2.1km (ignoring vague track off R at 1.5m/2.4km) and keeping L onto tarmac at T-junc-tion with BOAT at 2m/3.2km to T-junction by A685 near Wath at 2.1m/3.4km.

❹ Turn L, turning L onto C-road at next T-junction, forking R (W) at T-junction at 0.3m/0.5km and turning L at T-junction with bridleway track at 0.75m/1.2km to gate in Bowderdale valley at 1.1m/1.8km. Go SO, forking L at track T-junction at 0.15m/0.25km, forking L (S) round wall onto technical singletrack up Bowderdale at T-junction at 0.75m/1.2km to ford a rocky Rams Gill at 3.9m/6.25km (big climb starts now).

❺ Go SO up singletrack, forking R at 1m/1.6km on vague bridleway (W then WSW; easy to miss; if you end up at trig turn R and you'll rejoin route 200m WNW), forking R at T-junction at 1.6m/2.5km to follow obvious sin-gletrack swinging L round rim of

Calf Beck cove, keeping L at vague T-junction at 2m/3.2km on White Fell Head (steep descent follows; very slippery when wet; track near bottom is rough!) and swinging L across Chapel Beck at 3.1m/4.9km up to gate at 3.6m/5.75km. Go

SO, swinging R at Castley Farm, down drive, turning L at X-roads with C-road at 0.7m/1.15km, keeping L (towards Sedbergh) at T-junction at 2.5m/4km and turning L at T-junction with A684 in Sedbergh to start at 4.15m/6.6km.

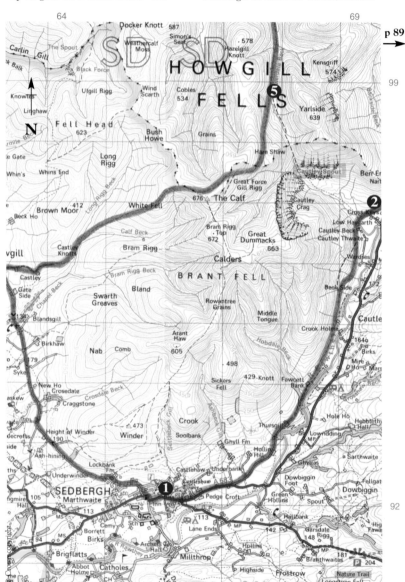

p 89 →

EXPERT Route 22
RAVENSTONEDALE COMMON

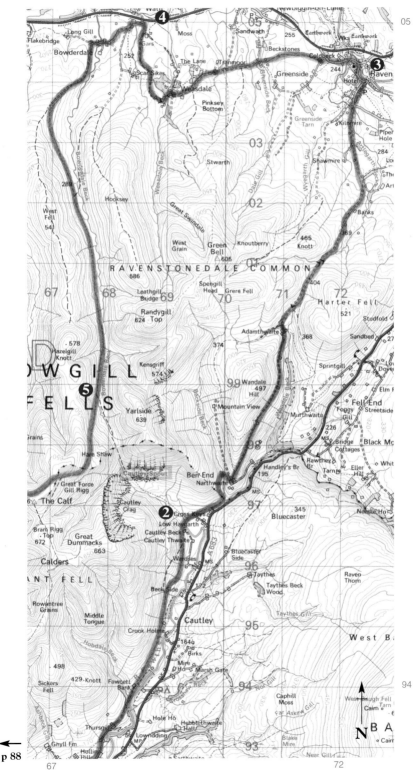

p 88

APPENDICES

WEATHER NEWS

☎ 0891 500 418 (Yorkshire)

☎ 0891 500 419 (Cumbria for Howgill Fells)

TOURIST INFORMATION CENTRES

Aysgarth Falls	☎ 01969 663424
Hawes	☎ 01969 667450
Kirkby Stephen	☎ 017683 71199
Pateley Bridge	☎ 01423 711147
Sedbergh	☎ 015396 20125
Settle	☎ 01729 825192
Skipton	☎ 01756 792809
YDNP, Grassington	☎ 01756 752748

YOUTH HOSTELS

YHA Northern Regional Office, PO Box 11, Matlock, Derbyshire DE4 2XA

☎ 01629 825850

Keld, Swaledale	☎ 01748 886259
Grinton, Swaledale	☎ 01748 884206
Hawes, Wensleydale	☎ 01969 667368
Aysgarth Falls, Wensleydale	☎ 01969 663260
Dentdale, Cowgill	☎ 015396 25251
Ingleton, Lonsdale	☎ 015242 41854
Kettlewell, Wharfedale	☎ 01756 760402
Stainforth, Ribblesdale	☎ 01729 823577
Malham, Craven	☎ 01729 830321
Linton, Wharfedale	☎ 01756 752400

BUNKHOUSES

Self-catering accommodation in converted barns with full facilities. Ideally suited for mountain bikers:

Barden Tower, Wharfedale (GR051572)	☎ 01756 720616

Dub-Cote, Pen-y-Ghent (GR819715)	☎ 01729 860238
Catholes, Sedbergh (GR653908)	☎ 015396 20334
Halton Gill, Littondale (GR882764)	☎ 01756 770241
Hill Top Farm, Malham (GR899631)	☎ 01729 830320
Grange Farm, Buckden (GR929780)	☎ 01756 760259
Skirfare Bridge Farm, Kilnsey (GR971689)	☎ 01756 752465
The Barnstead, Ingleton (GR686724)	☎ 015242 41386
School Bunkhouse, Chapel-le-Dale (GR746772)	☎ 015242 42327

Further information can be obtained by sending an sae to the YHA Regional Office (address given above).

OTHER ACCOMMODATION

The New Inn, Appletreewick, Skipton (The Dales' MTB pub in Wharfedale)   ☎ 01756 720252

BIKE SHOPS

Northern Dales:

Arthur Caygill Cycles, Borough Road, Gallowfields Trading Estate, Richmond. ☎ 01748 825469

Southern Dales:

Eric Burgess Cycles, Skipton.	☎ 01756 794386
JD Bicycle Workshop, Nelson Road, Ilkley.	☎ 01943 816101
Chevin Cycles, Leeds Road, Otley.	☎ 01943 462773

Western Dales:

Settle Cycles, Old Station Yard, Settle. ☎ 01729 822216

BRITISH RAIL BOOKING INFORMATION

☎ 0345 225225

☎ 0113 2448133

☎ 01228 44711

Stations are located at: Skipton, Gargrave, Hellifield, Long Preston, Giggleswick, Preston, Clapham, Bentham and Ilkley.

YORKSHIRE DALES NATIONAL PARK

Colvend, Hebden Road, Grassington, Skipton, North Yorkshire BD23 5LB

☎ 01756 752748

YORKSHIRE COUNTY COUNCIL

Surveyors Dept, County Hall, Northallerton DL7 8AH

☎ 01609 780780

CUMBRIA COUNTY COUNCIL

Highways & Transportation, County Offices, Kendal, Cumbria LA9 4RG

FOREST ENTERPRISE (NE ENGLAND)

1a Grosvenor Terrace, York YO3 7BD

☎ 01434 220242

THE CYCLISTS TOURING CLUB

Since 1878 the Cyclists Touring Club (CTC) has been the governing body for recreational cycling in this country and is recognised by such organisations as the Sports Council, the Department of Transport and the Department of the Environment. Membership is open to anyone interested in cycling. They currently have 40,000 members, 200 nationwide clubs and 100 local clubs affiliated to them.

Recently the CTC has taken on responsibility for addressing off-road cycling access issues which includes promoting Rights of Way initiatives wherever they occur and representing the views of mountain bikers at local and national levels. Local representation is done through a network of volunteer Access Officers.

If you would like to apply for membership then please apply to: CTC, Dept CSB/94, 69 Meadrow, Godalming, Surrey GU7 3HS.
Telephone 01483 417217.

Benefits of being a member include:

> Representation on Rights of Way and access issues in your area
>
> 3rd Party insurance cover
>
> Free legal advice for cycling related problems
>
> Free legal aid
>
> Free technical advice
>
> Free international touring info
>
> Bi-monthly colour magazine
>
> Free handbook
>
> Mail order service
>
> A voice in the world of MTBing

OTHER DALESMAN TITLES

Mountain Biking

MOUNTAIN BIKE ROUTE GUIDE: LAKE DISTRICT
Tim Woodcock £7.99

Walking and Trail Guides

LAKE DISTRICT, WESTERN FELLS Paddy Dillon £5.99
LAKE DISTRICT, EASTERN FELLS Paddy Dillon £5.99
YORKSHIRE DALES, SOUTH & WESTERN AREA Terry Marsh £5.99
YORKSHIRE DALES, NORTH & EASTERN AREA Terry Marsh £5.99
WHITE PEAK Martin Smith £4.99
DARK PEAK John Gillham £4.99
NORTH PENNINES Alan Hall £4.99
SOUTH PENNINES John Gillham £4.99
LANCASHIRE John Gillham £4.99
NORTH YORK MOORS Nick Channer £4.99
CLEVELAND WAY Martin Collins £4.99
COAST TO COAST Ronald Turnbull £4.99
PENNINE WAY Terry Marsh £4.99

Walks Around Series

BAKEWELL Martin Smith £1.99
BUXTON Andrew McCloy £1.99
CASTLETON John Gillham £1.99
MATLOCK Martin Smith £1.99
AMBLESIDE Tom Bowker £1.99
HAWKSHEAD Mary Welsh £1.99
KESWICK Dawn Gibson £1.99
WINDERMERE Robert Gambles £1.99
GRASSINGTON Richard Musgrave £1.99
SETTLE & MALHAM Richard Musgrave £1.99
HAWES Richard Musgrave £1.99
RICHMOND Richard Musgrave £1.99

PICKERING Nick Channer £1.99
WHITBY Nick Channer £1.99
KIRKBYMOORSIDE Nick Channer £1.99
HELMSLEY Nick Channer £1.99

Pub Walks Series

LAKE DISTRICT Terry Marsh £5.99
NORTH YORK MOORS & COAST Richard Musgrave £5.99
PEAK DISTRICT John Morrison £5.99
LANCASHIRE Terry Marsh £5.99
YORKSHIRE DALES Richard Musgrave £5.95

Dalesman Tea Shop Walks Series

LAKE DISTRICT Mary Welsh 5.99
YORKSHIRE DALES Richard Musgrave £5.95
PEAK DISTRICT Andrew McCloy £5.99

Safety for Walkers

MOUNTAIN SAFETY Kevin Walker £4.99
MAP READING Robert Matkin £3.50

Available from all good bookshops.
In case of difficulty contact Dalesman Publishing Company, Stable
Courtyard, Broughton Hall, Skipton, North Yorkshire, BD23 3AZ.
Tel: 01756 701381
web: http//www.dalesman.co.uk